LOST
DAYTON
OHIO

LOST
DAYTON
OHIO

ANDREW WALSH

THE
History
PRESS

Published by The History Press
Charleston, SC
www.historypress.net

Copyright © 2018 by Andrew Walsh
All rights reserved

First published 2018

Manufactured in the United States

ISBN 9781625859099

Library of Congress Control Number: 2018932112

CONTENTS

CONTENTS

PREFACE

In its heyday, Dayton, Ohio, was a center of ingenuity, innovation and invention, and the things made here, in a relatively small city in the center of the United States, changed the world. Many of the places that helped make Dayton great have been lost to history, while others have survived and adapted, representing the city's spirit of revitalization. Some of Dayton's distinctive and significant structures, such as Steele High School and the Callahan Building, were demolished, while others, including the Arcade and Centre City Building, saw hard times but now await redevelopment. Entire neighborhoods and commercial districts, such as the Haymarket and West Fifth Street, have vanished and show no traces of their past, while others, including the now-popular Oregon District, narrowly escaped the wrecking ball. Major manufacturers facilitated Dayton's early growth but later departed, leaving behind abandoned buildings and thousands of jobless workers. Other sites, including the Wright Brothers Factory and Huffman Prairie Flying Field, don't look like much today but once played a vital role in Dayton's legacy as a pioneer of aviation and national defense. And how many don't realize that the first NFL game was played right here in Dayton at Triangle Park? This book explores a diverse selection of retail, industrial, entertainment and residential sites that have passed Dayton by—as well as the influential people who shaped them—and reflects on the lasting impact they made on the city.

ACKNOWLEDGEMENTS

There are many people I want to thank for their help in making this book a reality. I thank the whole History Press team for their diligent work and guidance, including Ben Gibson, Abigail Fleming, Jonny Foster and Krista Slavicek, for initially showing interest in my ideas. As I was first immersing myself in Dayton history, Curt Dalton's many books on Dayton (as well as the countless resources he has put online) provided much inspiration, and upon meeting him, his advice and support were incredibly helpful. Aside from officially published works, a former UrbanOhio forum poster and blogger I know only as "Jefferey" inspired me with many well-researched posts that went into painstaking detail on many aspects of Dayton history. I also want to thank Bill Stolz and Dawne Dewey at Wright State's Archives and Special Collections; Nancy Horlacher at Dayton Metro Library's Dayton Room; John Gower at CityWide Development; Jon White at the City of Dayton; and Bob Smith at Sinclair for their discussions and help, along with countless other Daytonians with whom I've talked Dayton history and development over the last few years.

I also wish to thank my family for their help and encouragement. My parents provide a formidable support team, as my mother, Barbara, is an experienced editor and my father, Timothy, an accomplished writer. I first thank my mother for taking the time to review drafts and answer my many questions when I know she was juggling many of her own work projects. My father has inspired my writing ever since I "helped" him write his dissertation on many early mornings when I was a baby. And although I'm a first-generation Daytonian, I want to acknowledge my grandfather, the prolific writer John Evangelist Walsh, who researched Dayton extensively in the 1970s for a book on the Wright brothers published in 1975. As I was growing up, seeing him conduct research to write a seemingly endless series of books did much to awaken those same tendencies in me. I also want to thank my wife, Lillie, for standing beside me throughout this whole process and offering endless support.

INTRODUCTION

I'm not a native of Dayton, Ohio, but I've come to love the city since moving here in 2013. My interest in local history was, in part, inspired simply by looking around at the surroundings outside my apartment in the Dayton Towers complex just outside of downtown. Out of my sixth-story, west-facing window, I could see the popular Oregon District, Dayton's earliest neighborhood still standing. On the eastern side of my building sat St. Anne's Hill, an area contained in Dayton's original east out-lots from 1815 and the location of stately mansions and well-preserved mid-nineteenth-century housing stock. But in the middle of these two historic neighborhoods was something much different: drab single-story storefronts, wide-open green spaces and two large apartment towers, including my own. I wondered what development trends resulted in this unusual arrangement.

After I learned the story of what once stood on the grounds of my apartment building, I became fascinated by the ways in which Dayton has been radically transformed over the decades: buildings gone, neighborhoods vanished, industries decimated. The more I researched, the more interesting stories I discovered. It quickly became apparent that the concept of "Lost Dayton" had enough material to fill several volumes, so the question of selection came into play. I have attempted to choose a series of sites—be they commercial buildings, factories, parks or schools—that represent larger themes in Dayton's history and involve some of its notable figures. Some sites are considered among Dayton's

The Great Flood of 1913 was devastating for many sites explored in this book. *Courtesy of Dayton Metro Library.*

most prominent buildings, while others are somewhat lesser known but illustrative of something of great value to the city. I use "lost" to mean either demolished—as many of the sites are—or significantly transformed so that a location's original purpose has been largely forgotten. Many of the chapter sites interrelate, and one common thread is the Great Flood of 1913, which wreaked havoc on the core of the city of Dayton and devastated many of the sites explored in this book. Although the community rallied and rebuilt, additional forces such as suburbanization, deindustrialization and others forced Dayton to greatly adapt in order to cling to survival. The result today is a Dayton that has lost a significant portion of its character but one that has taken major steps toward reinvention for a new era and will continue to do so in the coming years.

PART I

NEIGHBORHOODS

1

BOMBERGER PARK

(The Haymarket, St. Anne's Hill)

The appearance of Dayton's Bomberger Park on the near east side has changed greatly over the years, but you can still stand at the top of the hill and gaze out over downtown. What you see in the foreground today, however, is completely unrecognizable from what was there before, as the area represents one of Dayton's most ambitious efforts to radically change the character of the city. Dayton's urban renewal in the 1960s destroyed a once bustling neighborhood that sat in between the Oregon District and St. Anne's Hill, two of Dayton's oldest surviving neighborhoods. And without a valiant effort at the dawn of the nationwide historic preservation movement, the losses could have been much more drastic.

Bomberger Park was the first public community center in the state of Ohio. It was named after William Bomberger, a businessman of German heritage who also served as a longtime treasurer of Montgomery County. One of his sons, George Bomberger, later become mayor of Dayton but died in office in 1848 at the young age of thirty-six. William Bomberger first arrived in Dayton in 1806 or 1807 and went on to own extensive property on the east side of Dayton.[1] He built his primary home on an estate just south of Fifth Street across from Dutoit Street in St. Anne's Hill, where in 1838, Swiss immigrant Eugene Dutoit built one of the finest mansions in the city on his farmland. The house still stands at 222 Dutoit Street. Bomberger's home, on the other hand, was demolished in 1908 and replaced by the public park carrying his name, which was financed by a $35,000 bond issue.[2]

Bomberger Park was originally part of a dense urban neighborhood. *Courtesy of Dayton Metro Library.*

The park building was constructed in a Romanesque Revival style, and the grounds included a large swimming pool and recreation area bordered by porticos as well as a separate wading pool. Bomberger Park provided much more than just a park, as it functioned as a major anchor for the neighborhood community. It had an athletic field, a playground and a field house complete with a gym, club rooms and baths. It even boasted a library, and in 1917, its one-thousand-volume juvenile collection contained both English- and German-language books, reflecting the enduring ethnic heritage of the neighborhood.[3] In later years, the building hosted community events such as dances for local youth.

The Haymarket neighborhood was built on the northern section of Seely's Ditch, a somewhat speculative canal that didn't end up finding much success. Despite its small size, the Haymarket had a diverse variety of businesses and industry in addition to elegant homes packed into its narrow streets. Early businesses in the Haymarket area included the Dennick Bros. Brass Foundry; the Schram, J., Horse Collar Factory; the Davies, S.W., Lumber Yard; City Steam Laundry; and a candy factory. The Haymarket's small, winding streets were laid out in an irregular pattern that must have contributed to a unique feel as one walked through the neighborhood.

The intersection of Fifth and Wayne, on the border of today's Oregon and the old Haymarket, in 1889. The Dover Block (*right*) is the corner where today's Dublin Pub stands. *Courtesy of Dayton Metro Library.*

Famous African American poet Paul Laurence Dunbar was born in the Haymarket, although the historic landmark known as the Dunbar House is located on the West Side of town at 219 Paul Laurence Dunbar Street (formerly North Summit Street). Dunbar actually lived in the nationally recognized home for only two years when he returned to Dayton in 1904. He had come back to live with his mother due to his declining health and separation from his wife, and he died in 1906 from tuberculosis. Dunbar's birthplace, though, was 311 Howard Street, a long-lost street that once ran parallel to Wayne Avenue to the east. That Dunbar home was located in what is today a parking lot behind the building at the northeast corner of Wayne Avenue and Bainbridge Street (across Wayne from the Dietz Block, the current location of Crafted & Cured).[4]

PEARL STREET

While Bomberger Park provided family-friendly fun, a few streets over in the Haymarket, a different form of entertainment thrived. Dayton's main red-light district centered on Pearl Street, which ran from East Fifth Street to Wayne Avenue. Despite its rather seedy purpose, it was well regarded by many, according to columnist Roz Young: "While admittedly the most sinful spot in town, [it] was generally a cheery place." Pearl Street ran for about three blocks but contained a wide variety of attractions. Young continued, "There were 38 brothels on the street, a cigar factory, a livery stable and the city hay market and weigher's office." Most of the brothel houses were large red brick Victorian structures, and many who walked down the bright, cheerful street admiring the elegant houses were unaware of what was actually going on inside.

The leading figure of the district was Lib Hedges, known as "the queen of Dayton's madams" or "the gem of Pearl Street." Born in 1840 in Germany as Elizabeth Richter, by the time she had reached her mid-thirties, she had settled in Dayton, and the husband she had met here abruptly left. She got started in business with a saloon located on South Main Street that offered glasses of beer for a nickel. But she also "dispensed other attractions in the back rooms at considerably higher prices."[5] This was a time when this breed of entertainment found its niche in Dayton, as some considered the city's other options to be lacking:

> *The movies and the radio had not arrived as yet. The old Victoria Theatre was virtuous and deadly dull; and the Casino, playing melodrama and burlesque, was just as dull and almost as virtuous. The local sporting gentry got an occasional kick when stranded carnival troupes showed to men only in the dingy upstairs fraternal hall on Jefferson Street.*[6]

The emerging brothels worked under police control, and each woman had to register with the police and take a physical exam in order to preserve Dayton's image as a "nice, clean town."[7]

DECLINE AND DEATH OF THE HAYMARKET

The Haymarket was densely populated, and the neighborhood as a whole soon started to decline. Although many today connect blighted inner-city neighborhoods to forces such as deindustrialization and white suburban flight in the middle and later parts of the twentieth century, they actually began much earlier. The seeds for large-scale clearance in Dayton were planted as early as 1933, by which time many aged buildings had already been demolished on an individual basis. That year, the city commissioned a housing survey that tracked larger areas in poor condition. The survey featured such designations as "vandalized units," "problem areas" and "illegal doubling up."

Accounts from these decades speak of urban blight as a disease and refer to targeted neighborhoods as "treatment areas," whereby "attacking" the problem of blight would improve sanitation, trash accumulation, odors, noise, overcrowding and related issues. Razing was recommended for areas where these issues were widespread, as "urban blight has advanced to such a degree that by local standards nothing short of clearance is practicable."[8] There was also a social engineering aspect to the renewal movement, which is evident in the 1933 housing survey itself in which Edwin Burdell, an Ohio State sociology professor, explained that "physical conditions of bad housing directly menace morals, health and economic independence" and that a crowded neighborhood "threatens a sense of decency and modesty."[9] In addition, racial and anti-immigrant biases were often suspected in decisions as to which areas to target.

The 1933 housing survey identified the Haymarket and an area on the West Side bounded by West Fifth Street, Broadway, Mound Street and Germantown Street as "the source of crime, delinquency and disease, comparable to no similar areas in the city."[10] The Haymarket specifically was called out for its "unsavory history," a street pattern that was "probably the most inefficient and wasteful in the city" and houses that were "old and dilapidated, many of which have amortized themselves several times…and 50 per cent…tax delinquent."[11] But the city recognized that the neighborhood was ideally located close to Stivers High School, Bomberger Park and downtown and recommended a plan that would replace the blighted housing with three-story apartment buildings facing a central park. This plan would also have preserved Eagle Street as the eastern boundary of the neighborhood, as well as the business district on Fifth Street east of Wayne Avenue. This first plan for the Haymarket was not executed. But two decades later, conditions had deteriorated so much further that stakeholders began considering even more drastic solutions, aided by additional federal support for a new vision for cities.

Urban renewal in the 1950s involved several interconnected pieces, and the federal government provided assistance in planning, regulating private land uses and—often most importantly—financial aid. Municipalities used tools such as zoning and housing and building codes to help make the plans work.

The overall plan in Dayton was to clear everything from Dutoit Street to downtown, and the first area to be razed was the residential area of the Haymarket. In addition, the area just north of Fifth Street would be turned into an industrial district. In 1957, the plan was submitted for federal funding, and it was approved the following year. In order to make such a massive project happen, municipalities need to acquire all of the properties in the area, and Dayton did so by 1961. At the same time, US 35 was being planned and constructed, representing another major trend with massive political support in those years: constructing freeways that cut through the heart of dense city neighborhoods. It was a movement that had profound implications for Dayton and cities across the United States, as highways cut off people from one another and from stores, schools and other community resources that are needed for a neighborhood to thrive.

The Haymarket is the most fully realized example of urban renewal in Dayton. It represents nearly perfectly the "towers in the park" vision of architects such as Le Corbusier, in which high-rises are built set back from the street to allow for landscaped green spaces. After the streets were cleared out, the Dayton Towers apartment complex was completed in 1963. Plans for a second tower and a low-rise complex were abandoned when the developer ran into financial troubles, and several years later,

Today, the Dayton Towers apartment building looms over much of the former Haymarket neighborhood. *Author photo.*

a different high-rise, today's Jaycee Towers, was built near the Dayton Towers instead. The result is an area that looks and feels suburban or even rural right in the heart of Dayton, here in between two of its earliest remaining collections of homes.

Roz Young summarized the idea that the Haymarket wasn't missed by many at the time:

> *It makes a sensitive person heartsick to see the wrecking ball of progress reduce a fine old building to rubble. Regret for what once was and cannot be again is no stranger to any of us. But when the area known as the Haymarket was bulldozed into crushed stone and splinters and finally open land by the progress of urban renewal not long ago, nobody shed a tear or raised a protest even though many a once splendid mansion of an early day was among those reduced to wreckage.*[12]

The complete destruction of the Haymarket can bring comparisons to other cities, including the Kenyon-Barr neighborhood in the West End of Cincinnati, a large African American enclave that was razed in the late 1950s for I-75 and an industrial park. The Haymarket was notably smaller, as Kenyon-Barr contained over twenty-five thousand residents, but Cincinnati commissioned an architectural survey just before demolition and at least captured what was lost in a series of 2,700 photos.[13] Decades later, Dayton started to document significant buildings that fell to the wrecking ball—for example, creating a detailed report on the Ecki Building on Wayne and Wyoming Streets prior to its demolition. But in contrast, very few pictures remain today of the Haymarket, forcing us to use our imaginations to picture the character of Dayton when its oldest eastern neighborhoods were connected.

Today, new development is planned just east of Bomberger Park in St. Anne's Hill. Fifth Street Brew Pub, the first co-op brewery in Ohio, opened in 2013 and has served as a strong community anchor. Building on its success, other new developments, including Dayton's first cat café, have also opened in the neighborhood, and more are in the works. In the former Haymarket itself, the Dayton Towers apartments remain popular, and expansive green spaces, once dense urban residential streets, surround the building. Across Fifth Street, the post office and distribution center built during urban renewal was planned to close in 2013 and shift operations to Columbus, but that has been put on hold and it remains open. Fifth Street east of Wayne once looked like a seamless continuation of the Oregon

District, and many hope for new developments in and near the former Haymarket in order to better connect the Oregon to St. Anne's Hill.

The destruction of the Haymarket had wide-ranging effects, but its impact on Bomberger Park itself is an interesting case. In 1955, a new $235,000 clubhouse was built to replace the original structure, which allowed the park to accommodate even more recreational activities. As a result of urban renewal, the park has actually grown in size significantly over the years, but it has lost its elegance and character as an anchor of a dense neighborhood and it's now adjacent to busy, wide Keowee Street. In 2012, the City of Dayton sold the Bomberger Center building to the Ahiska Turkish group nonprofit to serve as a community center. The Ahiska Turks are an ethnic group of refugees originally from the country of Georgia's Meskheti region who were expelled to Central Asia by Stalin in 1944 and later again exiled to various parts of Russia, Ukraine and Azerbaijan.[14] By 2012, 350 families had settled in Dayton, many fixing up homes and starting businesses, and the sale of the park building was in line with the Welcome Dayton city and community initiative focused on making Dayton an immigrant-friendly city. The city maintained operation of the rest of the public park, and the sign in front still features the Bomberger Park name despite the major changes it has seen over the years.

2

BAKER'S HARDWARE BUILDING

(The Oregon District)

I f you look closely at the southwest corner of East Fifth and Jackson Streets
in the Oregon District, you'll see a building that doesn't look particularly
significant. Most of the upper-story windows have been covered up, and
it's been given an interesting paint job. But it's thought to be the oldest
surviving storefront in Dayton, dating to 1851.[15] The longtime home of
Baker's Hardware, today it is a boutique hat and clothing shop. And more
broadly, the structure symbolizes the Oregon District neighborhood as a
whole—dangerously close to demolition but ultimately able to survive and
reinvent itself for a new era.

Today, East Fifth Street in the Oregon District is Dayton's trendiest spot
for food, drinks and entertainment, and it even earned national acclaim
as one of the Top Five Greatest Streets in America for 2015. You'll find a
nicely preserved collection of early commercial buildings, and the houses in
the streets behind East Fifth make up Dayton's earliest surviving residential
neighborhood. But at one time, it appeared that the Oregon District would
become another casualty of urban renewal like the neighboring Haymarket.

The Oregon District neighborhood was first platted in 1829, occupying an
area within Dayton's original east out-lots in pioneer settler Daniel Cooper's
1815 plan. It initially contained twenty-seven building lots bounded by
East Fifth, Jackson and East Sixth Streets, which were sold together for
$2,200.[16] That same year, 1829, marked a significant development for
Oregon and Dayton as a whole: the opening of the Miami and Erie Canal,
which connected the Ohio River to Lake Erie. This brought an influx of

Germans to the area, as many businesses were clustered around the canal. These immigrant workers lived close to their work and erected houses that reminded them of their homes in Germany.[17]

By the early 1850s, the area had started to grow, as it contained "seven groceries, three dry-good stores, two shoe stores, one hardware store, one drug store, two meat stores, two bakeries, two livery stables, three blacksmith shops, one jewelry shop, and eight churches."[18] Albert Marshall started a hardware business in 1858 in Walden's Hall and Block, which had been built a few years earlier at the southwest corner of Fifth and Jackson. John F. Baker, son of a German immigrant who opened the first grocery on East Fifth Street, got a job in Marshall's hardware store at age fourteen and quickly moved up the ranks. In 1874, he became partner, and the store became known as Marshall & Baker. A decade later, Baker bought out Marshall and took sole ownership.[19] During a time when many up-and-coming Dayton businesses shuffled from location to location, Baker stayed in the same spot for decades and became a prominent figure in the hardware trade. His was the longest-running retail business in the city when it finally closed in 1962.

The Baker's Hardware Store was the longest-standing Dayton retail business when it closed in 1962. *Courtesy of Dayton Metro Library.*

The origin of the name *Oregon* is a common question from visitors and residents alike, but it is not definitively known. It was presumably common by 1845, as an advertisement in a local paper offered "building lots on that part of the city known as Oregon." One theory is that it arose after the installation of an "Oregon Pumper" in the district's fire station.[20] Several early area businesses used the name, including the Oregon Brewery on Wayne Avenue and the Oregon Boot and Shoe Store at 510 East Fifth Street. The name Oregon, however, was soon be abandoned, and it would be many decades before anyone thought of it again.

The neighborhood's residential architecture dates from the mid- to late 1800s. A notable feature of the area is the juxtaposition of modest working-class families' dwellings and architecturally significant larger homes of Dayton's wealthier class. Prominent early residents included John Balsley, the inventor of the stepladder; William McHose, founder of the ornamental iron manufacturer McHose and Lyon Company; and Daniel McSherry, owner of the Dayton Grain Drill Works.[21] Tecumseh Street has the largest concentration of the earliest homes, starting from the 1840s, several of them built by Thomas Brown. Jackson Street is dotted with larger postbellum homes built for Dayton's successful businessmen. A modern-day visitor walking the streets can clearly discern the different lifestyles of the different classes of occupants.

Significant commercial buildings include the Balsley Building, a beautiful Victorian commercial structure built by John Balsley that has sat vacant for decades; the imposing-looking Ware Block, which housed a dry goods store in the late 1800s and today has many popular businesses, including Bonnett's bookstore; and the old Wietzel Drugs building, once a pharmacy, barbershop, delicatessen and laundry that is today the Salar restaurant. The building on the northwest corner of Fifth and Wayne once housed the Grand theater; today, tenants include a martial arts studio, a coffee shop and a restaurant.

Before the construction of I-35 defined today's Oregon District's south boundary, Brown Street—which today is the main commercial strip next to the University of Dayton campus one mile south of town—ran all the way to East Fifth Street uninterrupted and was a major thoroughfare in the city. In 1918, a major disaster on Brown Street was narrowly averted, although it still resulted in the destruction of five businesses. At approximately 3:00 a.m. on May 14, two flatcars and a freight motor were hauling rail up the Oakwood hill. The drawbar in between the motor and the cars broke, sending the two flatcars hurtling down Oakwood Avenue and then Brown

Runaway flatcars destroyed five Fifth Street businesses in 1918. The building in the left foreground survives as the Oregon Express, and Wietzel Drugs (*right foreground*) is Salar today. *Courtesy of Dayton Metro Library*.

Street. They traveled all the way into the intersection of Brown and Fifth in the Oregon before crashing, destroying five buildings: Nash Plumbing, Schafer Second Hand Store, Wah Wong Laundry, Cadillac Lunch Room and Ross Barber Shop. Fortunately, no one was killed, although the next day's *Dayton Daily News* front page reported that John Weddel, who was on duty at the Cadillac Lunch Room, was "probably fatally injured"—he recovered from his injuries.

As is the case with many other lost Dayton landmarks, the Great Flood of 1913 devastated the neighborhood and marked the beginning of a significant decline. The Oregon District turned into a rental neighborhood with mainly absentee owners, and the business district changed from a "mini-downtown" to a concentration of "tough bars." During the war and shortly thereafter, a large number of Appalachians seeking work in factories and tool shops arrived. Many once grand homes became bachelor apartments, and some were divided into as many as fourteen units.[22]

The urban renewal movement that erased the Haymarket (see the previous chapter) threatened its western neighbor as well, as the East Dayton Renewal Plan of 1957 called for the clearance and redevelopment of the entire Oregon District area as the next step. As it played out, during the 1960s, the Oregon District's residential stock was culled on a piecemeal basis, as many vacant homes deemed to be hazardous were demolished. The largest loss was 161 total housing units in the southeast corner of the neighborhood that were razed for the Park Manor public housing project. The construction of I-35 would also shrink the neighborhood to its current size by defining its southern boundary.

The neighborhood was considered one of the worst parts of Dayton and a hopeless slum, with its beautiful homes languishing in terrible condition. Every single house on Van Buren Street, for example, was painted a dull gray.[23] The Fifth Street business district continued to suffer, with the longstanding Baker's Hardware Store finally closing. But although the neighborhood had suffered some losses, most of it was still intact. A new plan, however, would put much of the area in jeopardy.

An urban renewal feasibility study was conducted in 1966 by the Chicago firm of Bertram Goldberg Associates, which also designed the Marina City complex in Chicago. The Goldberg concept for Dayton would be similarly grand in scale and purported to be a "living museum through restoration of a unified period of architectural style and scale to the original buildings." A blending of preservation and new construction, the design would have radically altered the neighborhood and demolished many significant buildings. Only about 125 structures would have been preserved and the rest razed, including all of the commercial buildings on East Fifth Street, Wayne Avenue and Patterson Boulevard. New buildings would have included two high-rise apartment buildings with 600 units each, "two sunken and lighted community malls with fountains and sculpture," lighted pedestrian plazas, hundreds of underground parking spaces and amenities, including a bowling alley and a library. But despite all that would have been lost, the Goldberg plan would have retained some of the existing street grid and many individual homes, a different proposition from the total erasure of the Haymarket. It would have been implemented gradually in phases, with the land acquired by 1971, surviving houses rehabilitated by 1973, the first high-rise built by 1977 and the second by 1982 and the city's financial share reimbursed by 1989.[24]

These plans were never implemented due to lack of funds, and a more grassroots preservation movement arose to rescue the Oregon. After seeing the neighboring Haymarket district razed to the ground, many Dayton residents started to fight back against such large-scale clearance projects. And at the federal level, the Vietnam War was starting to halt expensive urban renewal plans around the country, and plans for major clearance were abandoned. Locally, the City of Dayton was reluctant to commit financially to the Goldberg proposal, and a supplemental report from another firm stated that the plan was like "a well-designed car without an engine" and failed to take into account the social and economic conditions of the time. Many say that these proposed plans saved the neighborhood, because they brought widespread attention to it and inspired a collective spirit of preservation. Pioneers began to move to the neighborhood, buying up homes that would need a massive amount of rehab work. The people who moved in often had no running water, bathrooms, kitchens or heat. In 1973, neighbors banded together and formed the Organization for the Burns-Jackson Area. After two meetings, the group voted to change its name to the Oregon Historic District Society, reclaiming the name with so much historical significance instead of the meaningless Burns-Jackson (many neighborhoods received names only when city planners picked cross-streets within the areas they planned to demolish). The following year, 1974, the Oregon Historic District was added to the National Register of Historic Places, the first neighborhood in Dayton to achieve such recognition.

The rehab of the Oregon District was fueled by a spirit of volunteerism among the new residents—a group of neighbors broke up the asphalt on streets themselves to expose brick underneath, for example, as no city money was available for the effort.[25] Despite these pioneer efforts and a marked improvement in much of the housing stock, the general area's seedy reputation still persisted in the 1970s and '80s. The intersection of Fifth and Wayne came to be known as "Filth and Wine," a prominent corner in an area of sin, but without the bawdy charm of the Pearl Street red-light district a century earlier. Filled with adult shops and widespread debauchery, it was considered a very rough part of Dayton.

The rehabilitation of the neighborhood also fueled some animosity among the renters being displaced, although there is little consensus as to what extent this displacement really happened. The establishment of the area as a nice residential community was at odds with the notorious bars of the area, which by the 1970s included the Southern Belle and Fred and Sylvia's Tavern. In a 1986 interview, Sylvia Tincher, who with her husband bought the bar formerly known as Charley's, said that it "was a rough place, the kind of bar the working man came to," and that "you came down here to do your fightin'.".²⁶ This tension between the Oregon as a quiet neighborhood versus a rowdy nightlife and entertainment destination persists to this day and has manifested itself in disagreements over liquor licenses on East Fifth Street and parking. But in the early years, the tension was even greater due to the fact that these two bars were on Brown Street, right in the heart of the neighborhood, rather than at the periphery on East Fifth Street. Although they were often depicted as a danger, many of the new residents considered the area winos harmless. The bars remained in the area for many more years, as Fred and Sylvia's finally closed down in 1995 and was replaced by an antiques store and then an architect's offices. The Southern Belle moved to a new location on Patterson Boulevard in 2002, ending the run of bars deep in the middle of the residential neighborhood. The building was later converted to a luxurious residence by Dr. Mike Irvin, who invested over $1.5 million into the property after buying it for just $72,000 in 2007, when it was a "broken down bar with its roof falling in."

The Oregon District is largely intact, but with some key losses, and the general character of the neighborhood has changed somewhat. The site

The streets of the Oregon District are lined with historic homes. *Author photo.*

where Newcom School, which once served neighborhood children, stood is now a grassy park with a gazebo. The imposing church that stood on the northeast corner of Fifth and Jackson is now a one-story Goodwill, and another former church at the northwest corner of Sixth and Brown is a grassy lot. Other abandoned churches were saved, however: one on Clay and Van Buren houses swanky condos, and another on Clay and Cass was turned into the Urban Krag indoor climbing gym. And although plenty of nice restaurants abound on Fifth Street today, much of the district caters to visiting suburbanites, and places for residents to buy groceries or necessities are hard to find (especially after Fifth Street Wine and Deli moved out of its Fifth Street location in 2016).

Once, the commercial buildings of today's Oregon District extended far east down Fifth Street as well as north and south on Wayne Avenue, but most of this is lost today. A pocket of old buildings on Wayne Avenue near I-35 survived, including the 1886 Dietz Block that is today the home of Crafted and Cured, a craft beer and wine bar, and additional restaurants and small food shops in the adjacent storefronts plan to open soon under the name of District Provisions.

As for Walden's Hall and Block, after Baker's Hardware closed in 1962, the building was occupied by a shoe repair shop and an adult book store.

Only half of the Baker's Hardware building survived the Oregon's decline, but it has been reborn as a boutique hat store. *Author photo.*

By 1976, it still had tenants but was in poor shape. The city condemned the building as well as its neighbor, saying that the "collapse of the entire rear portion of the building" was imminent. This prediction soon came true, as a rear wall fell, making it likely that the entire building would need to be demolished. Although the Oregon District had recently been awarded historic status, the building owners had the option to tear it down without special approval because the city itself had condemned the structure.[27] Eventually, half of the building was demolished, but the rest was salvageable. In the mid-1990s, the surviving portion of the building housed Art Movies, which was owned by a company that also operated at least four other adult video arcades downtown, including two others on the same stretch of East Fifth Street. After several of those closed down, the old Baker building was vacant and an eyesore, until Dayton transplant Amelia O'Dowd saw some retail potential and stepped in. According to her website, the revitalization was a simple process: "In 2012 Amelia bought an ugly building, painted it yellow, and started selling hats." Her store is called Brim, and it offers hats for men, women and children as well as a variety of accessories. Despite the ups and downs encountered by East Fifth and the Oregon District as a whole, the building has come full circle as it is once again a specialized shop on a street that has reclaimed its commercial vitality. Today's customers, however, are just as likely to be suburbanites as residents of the neighborhood, as would have been the case in the old days.

3

CLASSIC THEATER, PALACE THEATER

(West Fifth Street)

The Classic Theater was a major achievement in 1926 for the growing black population on Dayton's West Side, and it was the first theater in the United States built and operated solely by African Americans.[28] Carl P. Anderson and Goodrich Giles, from Piqua, Ohio, recognized the need for a high-quality theater for blacks to attend, as segregation denied them access to Dayton's best entertainment facilities, in particular the downtown theaters. Anderson had learned construction from his father, and Giles was already a prominent figure in Piqua as the first local African American to establish a significant business (the Cottage Livery Stable) and the first to run for public office, which he did in 1886. Anderson and Giles set off to plan and build a grand structure for entertainment. They succeeded, as the theater "typified the middle 20th century with many Georgian characteristics. The ground floor of the five-bay facade is dominated by entrances."[29] The first floor was where movies were shown, and the upstairs ballroom housed the live entertainment. The theater had seats for five hundred people.

Another larger theater, the Palace, opened the following year, 1927, and over the next few decades, the stretch along West Fifth Street evolved into Dayton's black business and entertainment district. Major stars such as Duke Ellington, Ella Fitzgerald and Count Basie performed on West Fifth Street.[30] The theaters also hosted other types of events, including in 1940 when black students at Roosevelt High School, facing discrimination, turned to the Classic Theater's ballroom as a prom venue. That same year, children could

The Classic Theater, the first theater in the United States to be built, owned and operated by African Americans, was demolished in 1993. *Courtesy of Dayton History.*

go to the Classic to see a double feature, a serial, a newsreel and a cartoon, all for a grand total of sixteen cents.[31]

Today, however, you won't find any trace of these two grand theaters, or even any of the district itself.

West Fifth Street ran into a devastating combination of challenges starting in the 1960s. But even among stories of blighted neighborhood commercial areas, a common situation in the Rust Belt, this one stands out. In several cases in Dayton itself, blocks of buildings sit mostly vacant (Santa Clara Business District), while in others, demolition has thinned out the density, resulting in a few surviving structures interspersed with green space (Troy and Valley Business District). But West Fifth Street is different; nearly everything on this street has completely vanished. Multiple city blocks stretch by without a single building standing, the landscape returned to a rough form of urban prairie interspersed with an occasional boarded-up house waiting to be demolished.

How could this total erasure of a once thriving thoroughfare have taken place?

African American infrastructure grew steadily on Dayton's West Side, as blacks arrived in increasing numbers starting around 1870. The decades of 1910 and 1920 saw an even larger increase as the Great Migration from the South began. African Americans wishing to leave behind the discrimination and limited job opportunities of the rural South found a community in Dayton—numerous churches and black social organizations were clustered on the West Side, and segregated housing policies prevented most of them from settling elsewhere. By the 1950s, the West Side had become a thriving area for business and a cultural center for Dayton's African American population, with theaters, bars and many stores. In 1960, 95 percent of Dayton's black population lived in West Dayton, and by 1963, there were sixty-three businesses on West Fifth Street.

The business district centered on West Fifth Street came to be known as the "Nickel," and a stroll down the street, hopping between the many jazz clubs and cocktail bars, was affectionately referred to as "walking the Nickel." One resident described it this way: "If you were not seen on Fifth Street on a Saturday night back then, you were just an old stick in the mud."[32] Another Daytonian, James "Foots" Jackson, pointed out that although a streetcar ride in those days cost three cents, he never rode it. "I walked so people could see me," he explained. And on a special occasion like Easter Sunday, "The girls would put on their Easter bonnets and the boys would put on their best suits and we would walk up and down Fifth Street all the way from Summit Street to the bridge showing off our nice, new clothes."[33]

An account of actor Ted Ross described his patronage of the district: "He loved the clubs on West Fifth Street—Dayton's answer to Harlem in the first half of the 20th century. While in junior high, Ross, who was big for his age, would dress up and strut into the Owl Club and the Palace Theater's Midnight Rambles to see great acts such as Duke Ellington."[34]

And the Nickel was much more than just an entertainment destination. Its several churches added to the sense of community, as described by Sumlin: "Back then, I wasn't afraid to go anywhere. The people who owned businesses in the black community were also members of your church, so you felt close and connected. I knew all of the people in the community, the business that they ran and, they knew me," Sumlin said. "It's gone now—the warmth, connection, and the friendship."[35]

This way of life would come crashing down as the result of a few major events, and the area would never recover. Many would say that Dayton as a whole was forever affected. On September 1, 1966, Lester Mitchell, a black man, was shot and killed in a drive-by shooting on West Fifth Street by a white man who was never identified. This proved to be a tipping point for many already alienated black residents, and rioting ensued on the West Side. On that first day, 23 people were injured and 105 arrested, and 1,000 National Guard troops were sent. In the ensuing days, 500 people would be arrested. Riots continued the following year, and another catalyst was the 1967 killing of Robert Barbee—a local businessman shot by the Dayton police—a case that ended with an acquittal for the officer.[36] The riots resulted in the burning down and damaging of many West Fifth Street businesses. But other factors played major roles in the area's decline as well.

Freeway construction greatly contributed to neighborhood decline and abandonment, and the West Dayton area was hit doubly in that two interstates (I-75 and I-35) sliced it apart, with the former isolating it from downtown across the Great Miami River. West Fifth Street itself was broken into sections so that it no longer directly connected to downtown. In addition, some of the area near West Fifth, including Baxter Street—which was directly south of Fifth between Mound and Hawthorn Streets and once was the heart of the neighborhood—was removed for industrial development.

In later years, the Palace Theater, which had closed in 1967, was converted to new uses, as explained in one account: "In the mid-1970s this building housed the Ghetto's Palace Yoga Institute, led by Wally Ahmed Sababu. I lived there with about 35 other people in the lobby and offices, though the actual theater had been destroyed in a fire. We also had a factory across the street that manufactured and sold incense sticks."[37] But it was not long before it was shuttered completely.

Other prominent buildings on West Fifth also met their end at this time, including the West Carnegie Branch Library at 1612 West Fifth Street. The branch was discontinued in the 1960s and destroyed by a fire in 1979.

Additionally, an otherwise positive trend also played a major role in the area's decline: as overt segregation eased up in the 1970s, African Americans could more easily move into different areas, and they did, which thinned out the once dense neighborhood streets around West Fifth, once the only part of town where blacks could comfortably live.

By 1980, West Fifth Street was radically altered, but the two theaters still stood. The Classic Theater, which had closed in 1959, was added to the National Register of Historic Places, but that designation alone does not promise survival. As the theater's condition worsened in the mid-1980s, Dean Lovelace, who would later become Dayton's longest-serving city commissioner, formed a steering committee in an attempt to save the building. The city granted the committee two years to renovate the structure, and a study also suggested that it might be possible to keep the façade and erect a new building behind it. But the obstacles were too great to overcome, and by 1991, the theater was in terrible shape, as reported by the *Dayton Daily News*: "Pigeons roost on the windowsills of the Classic, the jagged edges of broken glass forming a ghostly design. Weeds have overgrown a wire fence the city put around the building to keep vandals out and protect pedestrians from falling pieces of mortar or brick."[38] The decision was made to demolish the building, as it was deemed an "immediate public safety hazard." Daytonians said goodbye to the Classic with an unusual ceremony: a public funeral that included a eulogy. Many people who had loved the Classic decades earlier gave speeches, and roughly forty people attended. The City of Dayton saved the marquee and promised to restore it on a new theater, ideally at the same location.

The Palace Theater on West Fifth Street was demolished in 2002. *Courtesy of Dayton History.*

But that never happened. The significant blow of the neighborhood losing such an iconic building as the Classic foreshadowed the fate of the rest of West Fifth Street in the following years—and perhaps sealed the fate of its neighbor, the Palace. Like the Classic, there were preservation efforts planned for the Palace. In 1996, Legacy Entertainment Inc. bought the theater and planned to turn it into an entertainment complex but failed to raise enough money. Then two entrepreneurs, Dennis Robinson and Michael Branch, announced plans to restore the theater and envisioned a grand reuse plan, including a seven-hundred-seat theater, state-of-the-art television and audio studios and conference and community meeting spaces. But the many millions of dollars required to first stabilize the building and then realize the restoration plan were unattainable. Robinson and Branch scrambled to assemble financing while they requested appeals and extensions from the city, as the property had been in the nuisance abatement program for years and was earmarked for demolition. Near the end, Robinson said that "all we need is a miracle," but unfortunately, his pleas weren't answered. The Palace Theater was demolished in 2002, and although its marquee was saved as well, by this time, there were no plans to restore the street to commercial use.

Specifics of West Side geography also made it tougher to save icons like the Palace on West Fifth Street. In the 1980s, when the only surviving Wright bicycle shop was rediscovered on Williams Street, that area, including West Third Street, became part of the Dayton Aviation Heritage National Historical Park, making it eligible for federal funding. But since West Fifth Street is outside the boundary of that area, the Palace was ineligible for those moneys.

In the 1980s, the West Third Street Business District came dangerously close to demolition, too, as part of a larger urban renewal effort, but it was ultimately saved, aided by preservationists and the long-lost Wright brothers connection. Today, there is some revitalization in the West Third Street Business District, still anchored by the aviation museum but with new restaurants such as Texas Beef and Cattle Company moving in and a proposed bike shop that would sell Wright-style bicycles. West Fifth Street remains barren, however, with one notable exception. The 1927 YMCA building at 907 West Fifth Street, built at a time when blacks were barred from the downtown YMCA, was purchased by the Dayton Urban League for its offices in 2005. Today, it is occupied by the nonprofit Miami Valley Home Opportunities and is the only major structure that survives. Years after both historic theaters bit the dust, so went the last prominent

Today, multiple blocks of West Fifth Street that were once a dense African American commercial and entertainment district are completely empty, save for a new community garden. *Author photo.*

commercial building, the circa 1891 F.M. Nipgen Building at the corner of Fifth and Williams across from the Palace Theater location. The two-story building featured a corner turret and octagonal roof as well as cast-iron detailing on its storefront, but it was demolished around 2012 when it was little more than a burned-out shell. The Nipgen Building also played a role in one of Dayton's most notorious crimes, as it was the location of the Short Stop Mini Market store where clerk Sarah Abraham was murdered as part of the 1992 Christmas Killings. Side streets in the Wright Dunbar area, however, are looking better, with infill housing and restoration of older homes making the neighborhood much more lively. The oldest home, the 1856 Daniel G. Fitch House, featuring Greek Revival detailing, stands at 105 South Williams Street. And a cluster of significant houses dating back to the 1880s can be found on Mound Street. But it will still take a lot more redevelopment before the promise of restoring the Classic Theater's marquee can one day be fulfilled.

4

KOSSUTH COLONY

(Old North Dayton)

On the quiet, unassuming back street of Mack Avenue in Old North Dayton, a row of homes featuring very similar construction line the street. They are modest, "simple gable-front residences with minimal setbacks, and asbestos siding covers many exterior walls in the district."[39] But the reason these houses are practically identical is not easily apparent when walking past at present day. Back in 1906, they were built as part of one of Dayton's most interesting chapters, an "experiment in the settlement of Hungarian immigrants" that was once called "the walled ghetto of Dayton" and a "miniature model city" in its own right.[40] The Kossuth Colony is long forgotten by many today, but during its time, it provided community, security and controversy.

Old North Dayton, a neighborhood immediately to the north of the Mad River and east of the Great Miami, was home for hundreds of new European immigrants arriving in the late 1800s and early 1900s. It was one of Dayton's early self-sufficient, walkable neighborhoods, with a mix of houses, factories, retail, churches and schools. The business center, at the intersection of Troy and Valley Streets, was known as the Point. By 1900, the neighborhood also contained four slaughterhouses, a boiler manufacturer and other industrial sites. But a train car manufacturer located in North Dayton would be the reason that the colony was needed.

The impetus for the Kossuth Colony came from one man: Jacob Moskowitz. Moskowitz was born in 1867 in Hungary and immigrated to the United States as a teenager in 1884. He first lived in Maine and Pennsylvania before arriving in Ohio, where he married Sally Baer in 1891. In 1899, Moskowitz moved to Dayton to take a position as a foreign-labor contractor for the Malleable Iron Works of Dayton, where he used his knowledge of seven languages and fluent command of English to recruit European workers to cross the ocean and work for the company.

Moskowitz successfully recruited over seven hundred workers from Hungary to the Malleable Iron Works in his first few years on the job, and the new arrivals settled on the west side of Dayton, where the company was located. He did much more than merely recruit these workers, however, as Moskowitz personally financed the construction of a clubhouse and general store to help transform the individual homes of these immigrants into something of a community. He soon became known as the leader of this burgeoning Hungarian settlement, now called the West Side Colony. Moskowitz's positive reputation spread, and he was recruited away from Dayton for a new position. But he kept his eyes on the Gem City and soon returned, now with an opportunity to realize an even grander vision for a self-sufficient Hungarian enclave.

For his second stint in Dayton, beginning in 1905, Moskowitz was hired by the Barney and Smith Car Company, one of Dayton's more prominent companies, which had been founded back in 1849. The company had decided to build their train cars out of steel instead of wood, which would require a steady supply of unskilled labor at the factory. From Moskowitz's early successes with Malleable Iron Works, the company knew he was the right man for the job.

By the following year, Dayton residents were surprised to see that "a miniature city had suddenly appeared just north of the Dayton City Limits." [41] Forty double houses were built in an area of roughly fourteen acres just north of Leo Street that was divided into two city squares of streets in the fashion of a complete small town. Immigrants, most of them Hungarian, came to the colony after seeing advertisements Moskowitz placed in East Coast papers, and he also made recruiting trips in person. By the end of 1906, about four hundred people were living in the Kossuth Colony, the majority of them men. Many of the married couples and families took in boarders, in some cases up to ten. Each boarder, many of them single men, paid ten dollars a month for their shared room, meals and laundry. A common evening activity in a Kossuth Colony home was reading aloud the *Szabadsag* newspaper, a Hungarian daily published in Cleveland. [42] Men rose at 6:00 a.m. to leave for work at Barney and Smith, and when the

Notre Dame Avenue in the Kossuth Colony in 1909, with the clubhouse on the left and the fence in the background. *Courtesy of Wright State University Libraries.*

workday was over, the group walking home looked like "a small army of men…trudging down Troy Street…like a flock of geese."[43]

The heart of the Kossuth Colony was the Clubhouse, a large two-story building that cost $35,000 to construct (significantly more than the houses, which cost $800 each). The Clubhouse served multiple purposes for residents of the colony: social hall, general store, post office and even bank. Workers wishing to arrange for relatives to come to the United States could accomplish this at the Clubhouse, in a small office selling steamship tickets. The most popular area of the Clubhouse had to be the beer hall, with five hundred seats and capacity for two hundred more standing around the seventy-foot-long bar. At the time, it was thought to be the largest bar in Ohio and was capable of tapping twelve kegs at once.[44] The store stocked just about everything, as it featured a large grocery, meat counter, dry goods, clothing and more. But colonists were required to shop at the Clubhouse for all of their needs. After cashing their paychecks, workers would trade in cash for special tokens emblazoned with the name "The North Dayton Store," and these were the only type of currency accepted. A guard even inspected incoming packages, and if they

Closing time at Barney & Smith Car Works, Dayton Ohio.

Men living in the Kossuth Colony were required to work at Barney and Smith Car Company. *Courtesy of Dayton Metro Library.*

contained items that could have been bought at the company store, they would be confiscated.[45] Moskowitz's offices, also in the Clubhouse, were "finished in oak and upholstered in leather," and they were private: any complaints had to be voiced at the cashier's office.

But the most prominent feature of the Kossuth Colony for those on the outside was undoubtedly the twelve-foot-high fence that completely enclosed it. This physical separation of the colony from the rest of Dayton raised an important question: was the fence there to protect the residents or to lock them in and exploit them? One justification for the wall was to protect workers "from raiding labor recruiters" who often had unscrupulous intentions. But was requiring workers to purchase all of their daily necessities from the company store exploitation? And was the isolationist nature of the colony damaging overall?

Although Moskowitz did find workers respectable jobs and ensured they had a safe place to live—in an era where crowded, dangerous slums were a reality for many immigrants—the twelve-dollar-per-month rent for a half of a double was considered excessive, and prices at the company store were also high.

The *Dayton Daily News* railed against the colony, portraying it as contrary to American ideals by isolating its members from the larger city. The newspaper played up stories of exploitation of residents by Moskowitz and relied on sensationalist tactics to make its point, even though it wasn't able to provide much evidence.

Moskowitz, in fact, invited the *Dayton Daily News* to visit the colony and see it for themselves, an offer that was not accepted. Nevertheless, the controversial opinions raised in the pages of the *News* prompted an inspector from Columbus to visit the colony to investigate labor practices. He found no violations. Although the *News*'s coverage was ostensibly against Moskowitz's practices, several of the articles suggest that the animosity was more against Hungarians in general, a claim that articles referring to "the scum of Europe" and arguing that "Hungarians are dangerous" strongly support.[46]

Interestingly, the competing *Dayton Journal* supported the colony and Moskowitz during this whole time, due to either genuine support or merely a desire to contradict the account of its bitter news rival. The *Dayton Daily News* even went so far as to claim that Moskowitz had acquired a controlling interest in the *Journal* for favorable coverage. Citizens' opinions varied, too, and letters to the editor published in both the *Daily News* and *Journal* echoed the sentiments of each paper.

For many Daytonians, however, the colony was simply seen as an entertainment destination: "On Sundays, whole families would come to the Colony, picnic-baskets in hand, to see for themselves the strange fenced-in settlement of North Dayton."[47] It sometimes got so busy that hundreds of visitors rode the Leo and Troy streetcar there on Sundays and "stared at the inhabitants until they felt like they were part of a zoo."[48]

The colony as it was did not survive the 1913 flood. As floodwaters swept through North Dayton, many residents escaped to higher ground, but a few were reluctant to leave. One, John Murin, had to be forced onto a rescue boat because he "refused to leave his loaves of bread that were baking in the ovens."[49] Others wanted to flee to safety but were left on their roofs and waiting to be rescued. The floodwaters, however, didn't go so far as to engulf the homes within the Kossuth Colony. But they did wreck the Barney and Smith Car Company, forcing it to close, and due to the nature of the colony, that was nearly as bad a fate. Large sections of the colony wall were damaged, with some even being taken and used as flotation devices during the panic. The wall would not be rebuilt, which would end the Kossuth Colony as an isolated company town with an employment requirement. Spared from the flood, the houses were left standing, and many Hungarians continued to live in them as they started work at other companies. Eventually, Barney and Smith reopened, and some residents returned to work there.[50]

The Kossuth Colony is long gone today, but the homes remain in Old North Dayton. *Author photo.*

Moskowitz sold the houses—some to their remaining occupants—as well as the Clubhouse and moved on to other business in the Dayton area. Today, the homes still survive and make up the Kossuth Colony historic district, which was added to the National Register of Historic Places in 1979. The clubhouse was demolished long ago.

In the middle and latter parts of the twentieth century, the rest of the once bustling larger enclave of North Dayton was reduced to a shell of its former self. The commercial center at Troy and Valley Streets, which was referred to as the Point because it formed a V shape, was cut off from the neighborhood it was meant to serve by Highways 4 and 75. Reuse proposals were particularly difficult because the other side of the river was turned into an industrial area, so little foot traffic would ever be achieved. The rest of Old North Dayton is not one of the nationally recognized historic neighborhoods but contains much of Dayton's European heritage. Sadly, much of the architectural heritage is gone and the ethnic heritage largely forgotten by many. Several buildings burned and were torn down before the vacant buildings in the Point business cluster were demolished in 2013–14. Nevertheless, isolated pockets of European heritage remain, including Charlie's Deli, Dayton's oldest deli; the Amber Rose restaurant, located in the 1910 building that once housed Sig's general store; and several churches. There is also still a Polish club, a Czechoslovakian club and a Slovak club in Old North Dayton. But the European population has dwindled significantly: one of the Hungarian churches only has four remaining members.[51] Today, the area is improving due to the influence of a new group of immigrants: the Ahiska Turks, who are moving into the area and rehabbing dilapidated homes.

PART II

INDUSTRY

5

NATIONAL CASH REGISTER

National Cash Register was the company most closely associated with Dayton and a dominant force in the community for 125 years after its founding in 1884. The earliest buildings of its corporate campus, none of which survive, were cutting-edge for utilizing an abundance of windows—80 percent of the buildings were glass—which made the production areas full of light and well ventilated compared to other factories at the time. This design even led NCR's buildings to be called the "daylight factory" during this period, reflecting a growing trend in industrial architecture.

The company that would become NCR had much more modest beginnings, however. James Ritty, a Dayton saloonkeeper, patented a crude cash register in 1879 after being inspired by the method by which ships tracked their propeller rotations and applying it to the recording of sales transactions. Ritty struggled to make a profit from his invention, however, as few shop owners saw the logic behind paying for a machine to do a job they could complete for free themselves. One of his few customers was local coal dealer John H. Patterson. Patterson took an interest in Ritty's cash register due to issues within his own company: employees were frequently stealing from the till, and that—coupled with inevitable bookkeeping mistakes—was enough to cause his store to lose money when it otherwise should have been profitable. Patterson recognized that these issues plagued merchants in many industries all over the country and that Ritty's invention had the potential to make a major impact, especially if he took it over. But the fledgling company experienced some early trials and tribulations before getting off the ground.

Above: NCR's factory consisted of dozens of buildings and occupied multiple blocks. The old fairgrounds are partially visible at top left. *Courtesy of the Dayton Metro Library.*

Right: NCR's cash registers were both functional and beautiful. Dayton's Carillon Historical Park showcases a splendid collection of ornate, elegant antique NCR cash registers. *Courtesy of Dayton Metro Library.*

Patterson bought two of Ritty's cash registers for forty dollars apiece, and with them, he quickly reversed the losses at his own store. In 1883, he decided to go all in when the company behind Ritty's patent issued new stock: he and brother Frank Patterson bought all of it. John soon bought out Frank and took total control, changing the company's name from the National Manufacturing Company to the National Cash Register Company. Then came the problems. The factory was in poor shape, as Patterson hadn't made an inspection before buying the company, and he also hadn't gone through its books. He soon learned that it was losing money. Plus, there was still the issue of nowhere near enough demand from shopkeepers to justify a major operation. But Patterson recognized that a solution existed to all of this: a dedicated marketing push to extoll the virtues of the cash register to shopkeepers and businessmen all across the country. He developed a legendary sales training program that would revolutionize how to persuade customers to invest in the new product.

Patterson was revolutionary in his systemization of the sales process. His brother-in-law Joseph Crane first wrote a sixteen-page document titled "How I Sell a National Cash Register," which Patterson used to formalize the sales training of NCR employees. The document became known as the Primer, and in it, salesmen were not only given scripts to memorize but also instruction on physical gestures to accompany the words, such as pointing to certain items when referring to them.[52] NCR's sales force spread out, covering designated regions and scrambling to meet assigned quotas. They were also strongly encouraged to get rid of the competition in their territories. The high-pressure approach worked, as NCR's sales skyrocketed from roughly 1,000 in 1886 to 100,000 in 1910.[53] But this sales team was hardly the only aspect of the company that paved the way for its increasing success.

In the mid-1890s, Patterson began a radical redesign of his factories that bucked most prevailing trends of industrial buildings at the time, many of which were operating in conditions that would have been considered sweatshops. The event that set this into motion happened in 1894, when a large shipment of cash registers was returned as defective because they had been ruined by spilled acid. Determined to get to the bottom of the matter, Patterson moved his office so he would be right on the factory floor. Upon seeing the working conditions up close, he wasn't surprised that his workers weren't overly concerned with the quality of their output, considering the dimly lit, monotonous atmosphere. He then hired architect Frank Andrews to "recast NCR in well-separated, steel-framed buildings with walls 80 percent glass,"[54] which allowed workers to complete their duties under ample natural

A busy day in the NCR tool room. *Courtesy of the Library of Congress.*

light. For the spaces outside of the factory buildings, Patterson hired noted landscape architect John Charles Olmsted to design attractive landscaping and establish gardens, sports grounds and a women's recreation area.

NCR's reconfiguration also went far beyond the physical facilities. Patterson also increased wages for his workers and added a number of amenities, including dressing rooms with showers, a subsidized cafeteria for meals, free medical care and more. His efforts weren't universally acclaimed, however, as critics accused him of paternalism. Companies today employ a variety of health-monitoring practices and wellness programs, but Patterson beat them by over a century, as he even weighed his employees every six months to gauge their health and gave free malted milk to those measuring in underweight. He also instituted exercise breaks twice per day for his employees, including starting the day off with ten minutes of calisthenics. This wasn't limited to the factory workers, as he also brought top NCR executives with him on early-morning horseback rides.[55] In addition, he purchased hundreds of acres of land near his factories and again commissioned Olmsted to develop them into parks

NCR's "daylight factory" buildings featured abundant glass. *Courtesy of Dayton Metro Library.*

and country clubs for officers and employees. In 1907, he debuted Hills and Dales as a country club for executives and later opened it up to all employees.[56]

As a manager, Patterson was prone to firing people, often impulsively. The NCR executive ranks were routinely shuffled as Patterson tired of his managers. He sometimes fired whole departments at once, and he let employees go for reasons such as "if they could not tell him why the flags happened to be flying that day or for not riding a horse properly."[57] He might have wanted to reconsider some of his layoffs—in particular, Thomas Watson, who after being fired from his role as sales manager of NCR in 1914 went on to found IBM.

Overall, NCR was much more than just a place of employment, as Patterson's community efforts went far beyond perks for NCR employees and had a major impact on a rapidly growing Dayton during the late 1800s and early 1900s. Patterson played a major role in the establishment of the residential neighborhood just north of the NCR factory, which became home to many of its workers. At the time, it was a rough area called Slidertown,

English Garden, National Cash Register Works, Dayton, Ohio.

John Patterson commissioned countless beautification projects large and small both on and near the NCR grounds. Here, the English Garden. *Courtesy of Dayton Metro Library*.

John Patterson was obsessed with his employees' health. Here, hundreds partake of a meal in the NCR dining hall. *Courtesy of Dayton Metro Library*.

with residents living in small shacks and shanties, and neighborhood boys, with nothing better to do, began breaking the glass windows of NCR buildings. Patterson responded by launching programs for neighborhood youth, including community gardens for the boys to work on. He also commissioned Olmsted for beautification projects in the neighborhood, including the grand Park Drive Boulevard. Today, the neighborhood is known as South Park. *Social Service* magazine wrote of the boys' garden initiative and its impact in 1902:

> *Boys who had been notoriously bad and vicious were formed into clubs and brigades, were given gardens and taught to respect themselves and the rights of others. Then people began to seek homes near the factory site, property rose from $300 a lot to three times that amount, and it is now by all odds the most desirable property in Dayton that is near a manufacturing plant.... There were forty gardens the first year, but the increased interest on the part of the boys necessitated seventy-four plots or gardens last year, each 10 by 130 feet in size.... The land, tools, seeds and instructor were furnished by the National Cash Register Company at their expense. Most of the boys supplied their families with vegetables during the past summer, and many earned enough money by the sale of vegetables not needed at home to pay for their school books for the entire year.*[58]

The 1913 flood, the greatest natural disaster in Ohio's history, was devastating for so many other Dayton businesses, as explored in the other chapters of this book, but its effect on NCR was more complex. In fact, in some ways it may have actually helped save the company.

In March 1913, after three days of late-winter rainstorms caused the Great Miami River to overflow, Dayton's earthen levees failed, sending floodwaters rampaging through the city. Up to twenty feet of water covered the downtown area, forcing desperate residents to their rooftops and the upper floors of commercial buildings, where they found themselves stranded. Under Patterson's direction, NCR rose to the occasion, building 275 rescue boats and sending employees out on them to bring countless stranded Daytonians to safety. (One rescue worker reportedly saved one hundred people singlehandedly, and Patterson himself, at sixty-eight years of age, went out on a boat to join the rescue efforts.) And the NCR factory buildings transformed into places of refuge for afflicted residents, as workers served meals to the hungry in its kitchens and set up a tent city near NCR grounds for those made homeless by the flood.

NCR's flood-relief efforts were a monumental act that played a major role in saving Dayton, but the company was also dealt a lifeline by the tragedy. Just prior to the flood, the company had worked itself into a precarious legal situation. NCR's ruthless tactics to stifle competition and undermine competitors got the company into hot water with federal authorities, who had indicted thirty NCR officials, including Patterson, in 1912 for violating the Sherman Antitrust Act. Patterson and his executives were sentenced to one year in prison. The company's heroic efforts during the flood weren't a get-out-of-jail-free card, but they did sway public opinion and may have played some role in the charges being dropped on appeal.

In the years after the flood, NCR continued its establishment of recreational facilities for its workers and made further contributions to the larger Dayton community. In 1918, Patterson gave 284 acres of the Hills and Dales country club to the City of Dayton, and it opened to the general public. Patterson passed away in 1922 at the age of seventy-eight, but in 1937, NCR continued his recreational legacy by building Old River, a 226-acre park for employees that included a massive swimming pool, a lagoon for canoes and rowboats and a playground for children called the "Tot Lot for Kiddies."

NCR remained dominant in its industry over the next few decades, but in the late 1960s, the shift away from mechanical cash registers resulted in new companies claiming market share from NCR. But NCR would pivot its business, in a series of moves that would spell the end of its once revolutionary daylight factory. In the 1970s, it diversified its product line, including "sophisticated retail terminals, automated teller machines, and computers."

NCR shifted to manufacturing electronic cash registers and, due to its size and influence, soon gained back the market share it had lost. The main factory buildings started to close, and the complex was eventually demolished piece by piece. The NCR factories had originated at the corner of Brown and Steward Streets, where the first building was erected in 1888. It soon exploded into a massive campus with dozens of buildings, many of which were all but useless now, as is evident in NCR's 1975 annual report:

> *We don't need the space or the diversity of manufacturing facilities which were formerly required.... [W]e can now produce...microcircuits not much bigger than the head of a pin, which contain up to 16,000 components. These replace mechanisms that required hundreds of individually machined parts and scores of space-consuming machine tools and manufacturing processes to produce them.*[59]

The slow, gradual demolition of the once thriving complex was demoralizing for Dayton, as the city watched its most important company shrink so significantly and visibly. Once the industrial hub of the Dayton community, the former NCR factory site is now open grass fields and parking lots on the University of Dayton campus. NCR Building No. 10, which was its main administrative site, was razed in 1978. The 1912 NCR Auditorium, "an invitation to culture for Daytonians,"[60] which started as the home of NCR's night classes and later showed motion pictures, newsreels, comedies and other entertainment for both children and adults, met the wrecking ball in 1979. To replace the old, the company built a new headquarters a bit farther south in Old River Park and continued to shift its core operations to electronics. This resulted in a massive reduction of its workforce. In the 1960s, the company employed twenty thousand in Dayton, but by the end of the 1970s, that number had been reduced to five thousand.

On June 2, 2009, NCR CEO Bill Nuti announced what many had feared: the company was leaving Dayton for Duluth, Georgia, in the Atlanta suburbs, ending its 125-year run in the Gem City. The company had continued to shed jobs at a rapid clip due to deindustrialization, and it actually had fewer workers in Dayton—1,200—than it did in Georgia at the time of the announcement. Nuti claimed the move was necessary for the company to remain competitive in the industry and recruit top talent. Locals questioned Nuti's motives, with Lieutenant Governor Lee Fisher calling it "shamefully irresponsible," but it wasn't the first time an NCR boss threatened a move away from Dayton. In 1907, John Patterson himself had declared Dayton to be "known now, and justly too, I believe, as the worst city in the state" and threatened to take NCR, which at that point employed 3,800, to the East Coast. The difference, however, is that Patterson was exaggerating as a negotiating tactic for achieving municipal reform in Dayton—he even projected slides calling out particular Daytonians as responsible for its failings, many of whom were in the audience.[61] Nuti, by comparison, was reportedly uninterested in negotiating terms for the company to stay, and of course, unlike Patterson, he did follow through.

The University of Dayton purchased and now occupies the remaining NCR headquarters site for its research institute. (It had started purchasing some of NCR's buildings earlier in order to expand its campus.) But its demolition of some of the remaining buildings proved to be controversial. One in particular, the Art Deco NCR Building 26, which was constructed in 1937, had a significant history. During World War II, it was used in a top-secret project to develop code-breaking machines to be used against the Nazis. At the time, the only two American companies with the technical capacity to take on such a project were IBM and NCR, and NCR won out due to the personal connections of employee Edward Deeds, co-founder of Delco (see next chapter). The University of Dayton purchased the building from NCR back in 2005 and soon moved to demolish it. The *Dayton Daily News* took a stance of preservation, filling its entire op-ed page with an editorial urging for the building to be saved and saying the planned demolition "has painfully exposed how vulnerable the community is to losing historic properties." As demolition was pending, the *New York Times* also wrote a story on the building. Nevertheless, it was razed in 2007–8. Other later NCR buildings have been repurposed by the university, including the former headquarters building at 1700 South Patterson Boulevard, which is today home to the University of Dayton Research Institute. NCR Building 28, built in 1952, is another major structure that was purchased by UD; today, it is called Raymond L. Fitz Hall. But the last building constructed during Patterson's lifetime, the NCR garage (Building 18), was torn down for parking in 2006 when Cox Publishing, owner of the *Dayton Daily News*, bought a former NCR property.

6

DELCO

Dayton was an early powerhouse in manufacturing, known as the "city of 1000 factories," and worked at a fast pace to turn out goods that were in demand across the United States and the globe. Large industrial buildings aren't as immediately impressive from the street as historic mansions or ornate commercial blocks. They don't as often get put on historic landmark registries, even though their contributions to our collective history are perhaps even more important. As a result, they often either get demolished with little pushback or become adapted to new uses, often with little understanding from the general public of their original functions.

National Cash Register is the most well-known company to have hailed from Dayton, but Delco is another Dayton company inextricably linked to John Patterson's empire that played a major role in the industrial history of the United States. And in contrast to NCR, its most important manufacturing buildings still survive and have been converted to new uses. No national historic markers, however, denote their original purposes.

In 1908, Edward Deeds, an employee at National Cash Register, solicited the help of his co-workers for a car he was building from a kit in his barn at 312 Central Avenue in Dayton's Grafton Hill neighborhood, north of downtown. Deeds had grown up on a farm in Granville, Ohio, just east of Columbus, and came to Dayton to take a job installing electric motors at Thresher Electric. But the following year, he left to join a growing NCR and set to work on designing an electric motor to power the company's cash registers. When he realized he didn't have sufficient expertise to perfect the motor, he hired Charles Kettering, an electrical engineer who had just graduated from the Ohio State University, to lead NCR's research lab. And it was Kettering who offered his assistance to help Deeds build his car.

What started as two co-workers merely tinkering around with car parts quickly turned more ambitious, as Deeds and Kettering started to work on an improved ignition system from what was available at the time. Deeds had recognized the potential for innovation in the automobile industry, once telling Kettering, "There is a river of gold running past us—why don't we throw out a little dam and sluice some of it our way?" Other NCR workers joined in on the project, and the group came to be known as the Barn Gang, which would eventually turn into the Dayton Engineers Club, an organization that survives to this day.

In 1909, Deeds and Kettering received a major vote of confidence in their budding invention when Cadillac put in a major order of eight thousand ignition system units. But the duo didn't have a factory and thought of themselves as more of a research and development operation. At that point, they didn't even have a name. They fixed the name issue by creating the Dayton Engineering Laboratories Company (Delco) and then scrambled to fill the order. Making the units functional was still a challenge that would take more months of tinkering. Kettering, confident of their prospects, resigned from his position at NCR, but Deeds kept his day job. Eventually, they got the job done, and the Delco ignition system debuted in the 1910 Cadillac. At that point, the Barn Gang moved on to what would turn into Kettering's signature invention, the electric starter, which put an end to the days of needing to use a hand crank to start a car. The men worked at a feverish pace for a year until showing off their progress to Cadillac in early 1911. The auto company was impressed with the demonstration, ordering twelve thousand starters.

But Delco still didn't have close to the capacity to produce those starters, nor did any of its manufacturing contacts. Grudgingly, Deeds and Kettering realized they would have to acquire factory space of their own. Delco's first manufacturing space was in the Beaver Power Building, which had just been built in 1910 at the corner of St. Clair and Fourth Streets. "At that time spec loft industrial spaces were called 'power buildings,' as they used to have their own power supply, at first from steam prime movers and belt systems, and later via on-site electric generators."[62] There, Delco moved its equipment from Deeds's barn and purchased new equipment in order to increase production capacity. The new company produced the first few sets

The first site leased by Delco for production is today the St. Clair Lofts apartments. *Courtesy of Dayton Metro Library.*

of starters in the Beaver Power Building but almost immediately needed additional production space. Fred Beaver was in the process of constructing a second space at 329 East First Street a few blocks north. Deeds and Kettering negotiated with him to adapt the building to suit Delco's production needs. The building was lauded as a well-constructed loft, particularly for its "dark brick-clad piers [that] soared the height of the façade, past narrow, light-colored floor slabs" that "illustrated the extent to which the grid[ded façade] could be manipulated for architectural effect."[63]

Delco needed to move fast to complete its Cadillac order, so it moved in and got to work before the building was even completed. The 1912 Cadillac proudly featured a Delco electric starter.

In just a year and a half, the original crew of 12 Delco employees had grown to 1,200.[64] As the company expanded at a breakneck pace, there were some struggles. Kettering was a brilliant engineer but lacked managerial acumen, so Deeds had to assume all of those duties. And during that already stressful time, Deeds was facing serious legal troubles: in 1913, he was among the NCR defendants facing antitrust violations in federal court. At age thirty-nine, Deeds feared that the verdict might put an early end to his promising managerial career. But due to the fortunate combination of appeals and the goodwill garnered during the 1913 flood cleanup and rescue mission, Deeds's name was cleared. Deeds also played a major role in recovery after the flood, including in the establishment of the Miami Conservancy District, the agency that built levees and dams and spearheaded other projects that would help save Dayton from future floods.

Once the legal worries were over, business proceeded as usual—at a booming pace. By 1915, Delco was producing around three thousand sets of starters every day, and another new building was needed to accommodate its operations. This new seven-story, 200,000-square-foot building became known as Delco Plant No. 2, located at 340 East First Street.

At this point, Delco electric starters were found in Buick, Hudson, Stevens-Duryea, Oakland, Cartercar, Cadillac, Oldsmobile, Jackson, Moon, Westcott, Paterson and Auburn automobiles. By 1919, Delco came to occupy entire blocks, utilizing a combination of its own factory buildings and repurposed older buildings. It invested in new ventures and community projects such as the Engineers Club.

In 1915, Deeds finally left NCR to exclusively focus on Delco. The following year, Deeds and Kettering sold the company to Billy Durant of the United Motors Company for $9 million but retained their roles as

Delco Plant No. 2 was built in 1915 during a time when Delco was expanding rapidly. *Courtesy of Dayton Metro Library.*

president and vice president, respectively. Two years later, General Motors purchased United Motors. Kettering assumed the role of vice president of GM's Research Corporation. The company that had started out as Delco splintered off into a dizzying number of new GM divisions, subsidiaries and related and acquired companies over the years, among them Delco Light, Delco Moraine, Frigidaire, Delco Brake, Delco Remy, Delco Products and more. Deeds and Kettering had launched other ventures even before Delco was acquired, and the Delco name also spread out physically to other locations within and far beyond the Miami Valley. Notable products from the 1930s include the cold carburetion system and the first dashboard car radios. Deeds returned to NCR and became its president in 1931, with his status as a prominent businessman helping to restore confidence in the company during the Great Depression.

During World War II, Delco's output shifted almost exclusively to the war effort, and it produced one million electric motors, twenty-five thousand generators, twenty-four thousand sets of airplane landing gears, forty million projectiles and fuses, seven million shock absorbers and much more for the U.S. military campaign.[65]

Over the next few decades, Dayton's many Delco and other General Motors plants led to its status as the third-biggest GM town after Detroit and Flint, employing at least thirty thousand local workers during its height. The story would eventually end with GM's departure from Dayton, which meant shuttered factories and massive job losses. As far as Delco, in 1995, GM discontinued the name in favor of Delphi Automotive Systems. This was a blow to many Daytonians, who took pride in Delco representing Dayton's status as an industrial pioneer. A *Dayton Daily News* editorial even suggested (perhaps in jest) that a Historic Names Commission was needed to preserve significant names like this: "You want to destroy an officially historic building, you have to get permission. You want to destroy a historic name, all you have to do is hold a press conference."

DELCO BUILDINGS TODAY

Deeds was also instrumental in the creation of the Carillon Historical Park, which today is the best place to get a glimpse of all of NCR's history that has been lost in Dayton, as well as much of Delco's. The 151-foot-tall Deeds Carillon tower, funded by Deeds's wife, Edith, was built in 1942 to honor the

Deeds family, and its fifty-seven bells make it the largest carillon in the state. A major park complex soon sprung up around the carillon, and it houses countless Dayton treasures, including the original Deeds barn, where all of Delco's work originated.

The Beaver Power Building, where Delco first set up a makeshift production space, was refurbished and converted to residential use in 2001 as one of the first apartment conversions in downtown Dayton's revitalization. It is known as the St. Clair Lofts and features 108 apartment units as well as ground-floor retail. The second Beaver Power Building, better known as Delco Plant No. 1 and today the Delco Building, still stands and today overlooks new neighbor Fifth Third Field, the stadium of minor league baseball's Dayton Dragons. After being abandoned by Delco at the beginning of the 1980s, the building, along with Delco Plant No. 2, were sold to the Mendelson family, who operate a liquidation outlet downtown. The Delco Building was subsequently used as storage space and underutilized for many years. But in 2015, it won historic preservation tax credits from the State of Ohio for conversion to apartments. That year, real estate development company Crawford Hoying brought a crowd of interested Daytonians into the building to see Charles Kettering's old office on the top floor, where "the aged windows [were] held together by rusty steel and surrounded by chipped paint. Kettering's floor has broken glass and even a dead bird still left over."[66] But construction soon commenced, and today, the old factory is known as the Delco Lofts, luxury apartments that opened in summer 2017 with restaurant and brewery Lock 27 on the ground floor. Plant No. 2 is still used by the Mendelsons for a liquidation outlet—it still employs an elevator operator to transport shoppers to the higher floors.

Other buildings were eventually demolished, such as Delco Plant No. 3, which was constructed in the 1940s. It was razed in 1981, and Fifth Third Field was built on the site in 2001. An underground tunnel under First Street that connected Plants 1 and 2 still exists.

As far as Delco as a former company, the name still survives in a couple of isolated places, such as GM's AC-Delco brand of sparkplugs and other replacement parts. GM no longer has any presence in Dayton, but fortunately, Delco's most important industrial buildings from years past have survived. Daytonians today who wish to live in the former industrial hub of today's Webster Station neighborhood have their choice of an increasing number of apartments and condos coming available, with the major Water Street multiphase development project also bringing commercial space and a hotel to the riverfront just east of the central business district.

7

WRIGHT COMPANY FACTORY

By most accounts, the Wright brothers are the most famous local citizens to have called Dayton home, and due to their extensive experimentation in various parts of the city, many local sites are connected to the duo. One of these played an important role in the history of aviation but has been largely forgotten and even physically hidden by surrounding buildings.

Before they changed the course of history with the advent of flight, Wilbur and Orville Wright dedicated themselves to making bicycles, and they worked in six different shops as they made their transition from ground to air transportation. The fates of these shops as well as the other Wright brothers historic locations vary. Some buildings survive but are no longer in Dayton, namely, the Wright house that stood at 7 Hawthorn Street, and the Wright bicycle shop that occupied 1127 West Third Street, which were both moved to Dearborn, Michigan, by Henry Ford in 1936 (a faithful replica of the shop can be found in Carillon Historical Park, however).

Their first shop, on 1005 West Third Street, which the Wrights occupied upon starting their bicycle business in 1892, was later heavily altered and incorporated into a larger building that became home to the Gem City Ice Cream Company. The building still stands but is deteriorating and in danger of being demolished. The second and third shops, as well as the fifth, which served as a showroom, have been demolished. The only Wright brothers bicycle shop remaining in Dayton close to its original form is the fourth, at 22 South Williams Street, which today forms part of the Dayton Aviation Heritage National Historical Park in the West Third Street Business District.

Left: The sixth Wright Bicycle Shop, which stood at 1127 West Third Street, is in Dearborn, Michigan, today. *Courtesy of the Dayton Metro Library*.

Below: A bicycle balances in front of the Wright home at 7 Hawthorn Street, which is today in Dearborn, Michigan. *Courtesy of the Library of Congress*.

The Wrights worked at the South Williams Street shop from 1895 to 1897, a period in which they launched their own bicycle brands and also began to apply their expertise to the emerging world of aviation. The building was blighted and slated for demolition in 1980 until a journal article about the Wrights by Fred Fisk and Marlin Todd featured a historic photograph of the shop, which inspired a group called Aviation Trail Inc. to purchase the property and rehabilitate it.

The transplanted shop was the Wrights' sixth location and where they began to focus their energies on producing a viable airplane, first using kites, then manned gliders and eventually powered machines, overcoming challenges every step of the way. They earned worldwide adoration for conquering the problem of human flight. Their six bicycle shops don't tell the whole story of the Wright brothers' forays into manufacturing, however. Ever industrious, they would attempt to do much more once the production and selling of the airplane became a reality. In 1909, six years after they achieved the first powered flight, Wilbur and Orville established the Wright Company in order to develop new flyers. Their need for aircraft production space now drastically exceeded the capacity of their earlier bicycle shops. They set up a production facility in a wing of the Speedwell Motor Company in early 1910. Later that year, they chose a location to set up a permanent factory, the first in the country built to manufacture airplanes.

The Wright Company Factory hummed with activity the first few years, with the first airplane sold to a Robert J. Collier for the sum of $5,000. The company established three divisions: government, civilian and flying. But the factory did not last long, as the Wrights ceased operations in 1915 after manufacturing only 120 airplanes. Wilbur's death in 1912 certainly put a damper on the operation, and Orville sold his stake in the company just three years later.

General Motors purchased the factory in 1919, and the surrounding area soon grew into a sprawling fifty-four-acre plant for automobile manufacturing, with 1.2 million square feet and twenty different office buildings. Over the years, the original Wright Company factory buildings became so integrated into the larger complex that they were largely forgotten. Later known as the GM Inland factory and the Delphi Home Avenue Plant, the complex officially closed in 2008. The vacant auto plant was demolished, except for a narrow row that included the two Wright Company buildings. Their reemergence among the rubble of the other buildings surprised many. But the buildings weren't out of the woods yet, as officials estimated that $4 million would be required to save the factory and turn it into a part of the

The Wright Company Factory buildings in 1911. *Courtesy of the Library of Congress.*

Dayton Aviation Heritage National Park. Several players, including the nonprofit National Aviation Heritage Alliance (NAHA), the City of Dayton and the State of Ohio, attempted to raise the money over the next few years. On June 20, 2016, the Dayton Metro Library announced that it had selected the Wright Company Factory site as the location for its new West Branch. The library would occupy seven acres of the site and consolidate two other west side branches into a larger facility. Having a brand-new library as a next-door neighbor would certainly help the redevelopment prospects of the Wright brothers' factory site. But the library plan has not moved forward due to an inability to reach a deal with the land owner. NAHA continues to raise funds for restoration of the Wright Company Factory and hopes to move toward opening to the public.

Building airplanes, of course, was only one part of the equation for Wilbur and Orville, as years earlier much testing and experimentation were required before the Wright brothers were able to achieve flight. Kitty Hawk, North Carolina, is the site associated with the achievement of flight, but the most important work was done at home in Dayton on another site that is today forgotten by many.

8

HUFFMAN PRAIRIE FLYING FIELD

In the shadow of the massive Wright Patterson Air Force Base and its main public attraction, the Air Force Museum, sits a site that was crucial to early aviation history but is regularly bypassed by visitors in favor of the impressive aircraft in the indoor hangars. Many rightly think of Kitty Hawk, North Carolina, as the location of the first powered flight, but the first "practical" airplane was flown right here in Dayton at the Huffman Prairie Flying Field. The Wright brothers achieved the first powered flight in 1903 at Kitty Hawk, a location they selected due to its windy conditions and abundance of open, sandy spaces. After they had cleared that first major hurdle, much further testing and tweaking was needed to make the new technology viable. The Wrights were looking to fly closer to home at a suitable location, and one possibility emerged in the spring of 1904: a cow pasture owned by Dayton banker Torrence Huffman. The field was located eight miles away from the Wrights' home at 7 Hawthorn Street in West Dayton, a quick ride on the interurban rail. Wilbur described the field in a letter to Octave Chanute, a French-born aviation pioneer with whom the brothers corresponded frequently in the first decade of the twentieth century:

> We are in a large meadow of about 100 acres. It is skirted on the west and north by trees. This not only shuts off the wind somewhat, but gives a slight downward trend. However, this is a matter we do not consider anything serious. The greater troubles are the facts that in addition to the cattle there have been a dozen or more horses in the pasture and as it is surrounded by

barbwire fencing we have been at much trouble to get them safely away before making any trials. Also, the ground is an old swamp and is filled with grassy hummocks some six inches high, so that it resembles a prairie dog town.[67]

This vivid description might not make the pasture seem particularly special as a place to fly, but Huffman's field fit the bill, as it was convenient to get to but still somewhat isolated. This was an advantage, since reporters had badly twisted the facts surrounding the Wrights' first flight at Kitty Hawk, and the brothers were hoping to better control their publicity moving forward as well as protect the secrets of their machines. Orville also had a personal connection to the field, as he had traveled to the Huffman prairie on field trips while attending Central High School in Dayton.

In 1904, Huffman agreed to allow the Wrights to use his field for their flight tests without charging them rent, the only condition being that they had to clear out the cows and horses before conducting any flights. Huffman wasn't too optimistic that the site would allow the brothers to do anything revolutionary, as he told a nearby farmer that "they're fools."

The 1904 flyer was nearly identical to the 1903 version, and the minor alterations the brothers made did not improve performance. In 1905, they improved on the first two flyers with a larger elevator and rudder that were both moved farther from the center of gravity. "This increased the torque produced by the control surface and provided greater control."[68]

This 1905 Wright Flyer III became known as "the world's first practical airplane," and in 1905, the Wrights achieved 262 minutes of flight in 50 attempts at Huffman Prairie (the previous year's Wright Flyer II stayed in the air for only 49 minutes across 105 flights). During these flights, the Wrights turned with ease, flew in circles and could stay in the air until their fuel ran out, massive improvements on their marginally controlled flights at Kitty Hawk. On October 5, 1905, Wilbur achieved a world record of over twenty-four miles flown in 39 minutes.[69]

Years later, after shopping their flyer to U.S. and European governments and dazzling the world with a series of public demonstrations, the Wrights launched a new venture called the Wright Flying School at Huffman Prairie, where they would go on to train more than one hundred pilots, including H.H. (Hap) Arnold, who would later go on to head the U.S. Air Force during World War II.

In 1917, after the United States entered World War I, the U.S. Army Signal Corps took over the Huffman Prairie field and combined it with

The Wright Brothers with the Wright Flyer II at Huffman Prairie Flying Field in 1904. *Courtesy of the Library of Congress.*

a much larger surrounding area to form Wilbur Wright Field. Edward Deeds of Delco and NCR fame played a pivotal role in the war effort. He helped form the Dayton-Wright Company, which manufactured airplanes; purchased the land that would become McCook Field; and later joined the army as colonel and chief of aircraft production. In this role, he worked on warplane engine design and also established both Wilbur Wright Field and McCook Field as hubs for army aircraft research.

Thirty-one years later, Wilbur Wright Field would be combined yet again with the adjacent Patterson Field to become the Wright-Patterson Air Force Base, which is the largest single-site employer in the state of Ohio, with over twenty-seven thousand employees. The original Huffman Prairie Flying Field, within the boundaries of the base, is today part of the National Aviation Heritage Area, separated by a fence from the rest of the base. It can be accessed through a dedicated entrance. The National Park Service maintains the field by keeping the grass short to simulate the old pastureland. It also features a replica of the hangar and launching catapult used by the Wrights in 1905. An interpretive center facility two miles away on a hilltop overlooking the field also offers exhibits on Wright and aviation history. But nevertheless, the field site is unknown by many native Daytonians as well as visitors to the Air Force Museum.

DAYTON MOTOR CAR COMPANY HISTORIC DISTRICT

Dayton was an influential automobile manufacturing city in its heyday, enough to earn it the nickname of "Little Detroit." A well-known story in contemporary times is the closing of the former GM assembly plant in Moraine, just south of the city limits, which closed in 2008, resulting in thousands of lost jobs. The blighted plant was given new life in 2013 when it was purchased by Fuyao, a Chinese auto glass company, for its U.S. headquarters. But many other locations around Dayton contributed to the city's auto legacy in the earlier years of the twentieth century. One is the Dayton Motor Car Company Historic District, a collection of buildings in an industrial area just to the east of downtown. The area leaves few clues as to the thriving businesses that once occupied the area.

What is now called the Dayton Motor Car Company Historic District actually predates the automobile, as the buildings there were originally used for a different purpose. In 1875, the Stoddard Manufacturing Company, located around Third, Bainbridge and Bacon Streets, was the largest farm implement company in Dayton and helped establish the city as a leader in the production of tools such as grain drills and horse rakes. John Williams Stoddard, son of pioneer settler and prominent lawyer Henry Stoddard, practiced law in Dayton for two years before leaving the field for a career in business. In 1862, he started a linseed oil business with a partner, which later expanded to paints, oils and window glass. After Stoddard sold his stake in the company, called Stoddard & Grimes, it later became part of the Lowe Brothers Paint Company. Stoddard turned his attention to agricultural implements in 1869, working with John Dodds under the company name of John Dodds & Company. At the start, the company specialized in horsehair rakes, and its property at Third and Bainbridge consisted of several frame shop buildings. Those buildings met their end in an 1873 fire, and replacements were built with brick to prevent a similar fate.

In 1882, the company employed some 450 workers. By 1889, the factory took up an entire square, with frontage on four streets. Buildings ranged from one to four stories and were powered by two 250-horsepower steam engines. Its location right next to the railroad tracks was ideal for shipping and receiving goods. Some of Stoddard's popular products included the Tiger Front-Cut Mower, the Climax Pulverizing Disc Harrow and the Triumph Broad Cast Seeder and Cultivator.[70] For its farm implements alone, the Stoddard Manufacturing Company earned a prominent role in Dayton's industrial legacy, as it was said to have "conferred a boon to the city in the advancement of its fame as a manufacturing center."[71] But it would soon branch out into other ventures.

In the mid-1890s, the company capitalized on a nationwide craze and began to manufacture bicycles, during the very same years Wilbur and Orville Wright were doing so on the other side of town. By 1903, John Stoddard, now working with his son Charles, had made a fortune with farm implements, and the bicycle experiment had spurred a broader interest in

The two main buildings near Third and Bainbridge were a hub of activity for Stoddard's agricultural implement production in the late 1800s. *Courtesy of Dayton Metro Library.*

transportation. This was strengthened by Stoddard's roles as secretary of the Third Street Railway and vice president of a Toledo wagon manufacturer. In 1905, he even sent Charles to Europe to study auto production. All of this led to a radical shift for Stoddard's company, as it moved into automobile manufacturing, becoming Dayton's first in that emerging industry. The new company became Dayton Motor Car Company and quickly doubled the size of its factory at Third and Bainbridge to over a dozen buildings.

The company produced the Stoddard-Dayton automobile and "had a reputation of quality cars and powerful engines and raced successfully in sprints, hill climbs and dirt races."[72] The 1906 Stoddard limousine had a thirty-five-horsepower engine and cost $3,200. Five years later, the company had expanded its production to twenty different models, such as the Stoddard-Dayton Knight, which boasted a six-cylinder, seventy-horsepower engine and a price tag of $6,250.

A 1910 magazine advertisement touted a diverse selection, including "touring cars, roadsters, runabouts, town cars, landaulets and limousines," all equipped with valve-in-head motors. Another ad touted the Stoddard-Dayton as "a practically noiseless car" compared to competitors that "sound like a boiler shop on a busy day."

A Stoddard-Dayton car also won the very first race held at the Indianapolis Motor Speedway, which had just opened in 1909 as the first proper speedway ever built. The inaugural five-mile race was won by Louis Schwitzer, chief engineer at Stoddard-Dayton, who averaged a speed of 57.3 miles per hour. Another Stoddard-Dayton served as a pace car during the first Indianapolis 500 in 1911. And the Indianapolis Motor Speedway had other Dayton connections, including in June 1910, when the Wright brothers came to town for a demonstration showcasing their latest Wright Flyers.

Several explanations have been given for the abrupt end to the Dayton Motor Car Company after about a decade in business. One is the fact that Stoddard-Dayton cars were expensive to produce in comparison to the Ford and GM cars that were starting to be mass-produced in Detroit. Some say the company didn't innovate fast enough as the car became a realistic pursuit for ordinary citizens. The other reason was the flood of 1913, which damaged the factory and destroyed designs, plans and other important company property. The company had merged with Benjamin Briscoe's United States Motor Company in 1912, but this did not improve its fortunes, and some say it hastened its demise. The company failed in bankruptcy in 1913.

The Dayton Motor Car Company was far from the only auto manufacturer in town—others included the Speedwell Motor Car Company,

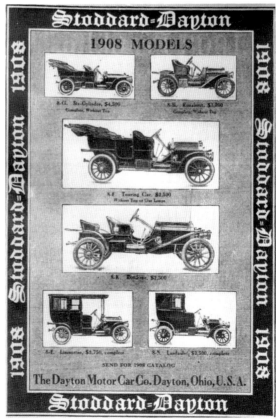

Above: By the time it had transitioned into auto manufacturing, Stoddard's company had expanded into a sprawling campus. *Courtesy of Dayton Metro Library.*

Right: Stoddard-Dayton's 1908 models included the Runabout, the Touring Car, the Limousine and the Landaulet, ranging in price from $1,700 to $4,500. *Courtesy of Dayton Metro Library.*

the Apple Automobile Company and Dayton Electric, an early electric car manufacturer. But the fate of the first automobile manufacturing facility in Dayton, as well as the industry as a whole, would be mixed over the ensuing decades. After the bankruptcy of U.S. Motors, the company was taken over by the Maxwell Motor Company. It stopped manufacturing complete automobiles at the Dayton plant but continued producing parts. In 1925, the company became part of Chrysler, which hastily shifted operations to Detroit over the next few years, effectively ending the era of home-grown auto production in Dayton. Of course, the sprawling GM plants of the next generation would enhance Dayton's overall reputation as a major auto manufacturing city.

A Packard dealership on 420 South Ludlow Street was constructed in 1917 and survives today as America's Packard Museum, which features a great collection of classic Packard cars. It has won several awards as a top auto museum. Despite being called America's Packard Museum, the official name is that of the original dealership: the Citizens Motorcar Company.

In 1984, a large area where Stoddard's businesses operated became a historic district, albeit one that's unknown to a majority of Daytonians. As with other buildings, such as the Classic and Palace Theaters, historic

This building, constructed around 1886 and used for storage and machine work, still bears the Stoddard name. *Author photo.*

recognition does not guarantee survival. A sixty-eight-thousand-square-foot building at 11 McDonough Street near East Third dating to the earliest days of the farm implement company in the 1870s was in dire straits in 1994. Kenneth Schriber bought the building in 1986 and invested $250,000 to restore it. In 1993, it suffered vandalism by squatters, who set a fire on the fifth floor that destroyed the building's roof. Schriber estimated that rehab would cost $600,000, and the city's Landmarks Commission allowed its demolition on economic hardship grounds. "That was such a good building and it stood such a long time," Schriber said at the time. "It's a damn shame. But it became apparent the risk [of further restoration] would be too great."[73] A seven-story reinforced concrete building that stood next to it at 15 Bacon Street—featuring large windows letting in lots of natural light, built shortly after John H. Patterson debuted that style for NCR's factories—has also been demolished. That building was used for assembling, trimming and painting automobiles. But a survivor, 15 McDonough Street, is another seven-story, eighty-five-thousand-square-foot building similar in form to the Bacon Street building and was constructed around 1908. It was used as a machine shop, a tool room and an assembly room for cars and had office spaces on the second floor. Several other early buildings along Bacon, McDonough and Bainbridge Streets remain.

This two-story warehouse dating back to the 1880s became the Union Storage Company in 1903, likely storing many Stoddard and Dayton Motor Car products over the years. *Author photo.*

Several of the buildings that survive in the Dayton Motor Car Company Historic District may be in poor shape today, but the surrounding area as a whole is seeing a push for redevelopment. Several companies still occupy buildings in the district, most notably machine tool and manufacturing solutions firm Gosiger, which has been family owned and operated for ninety years. And due to the area's proximity to the Oregon District and downtown, it has attracted developer interest for the structures that currently sit vacant or underutilized. Louisville-based Weyland Ventures restored the old Weustoff and Getz building at 210 Wayne Avenue into forty apartments, and the company envisions a dozen potential projects in the area it dubbed Oregon East, including former motor car buildings. The developers are first hoping to convert 15 McDonough Street into modern offices with lots of open space. Although the days of farm implements or luxury cars being produced in these buildings are long gone, there's hope the area can be turned into a thriving mixed-use district. And as for the long-lost Stoddard-Dayton automobile, a 1908 model now resides in Carillon Historical Park after Charles Kettering's son Eugene put up $15,000 to buy it from a local owner in 1967.[74]

PART III

RETAIL

10

DAYTON ARCADE

The Dayton Arcade was a prominent fixture of downtown for many decades, so iconic as to earn it the moniker of the "Crown Jewel of the Gem City." But the story of the complex of five interconnected buildings is not, as some assume, one of initial popularity followed by gradual decline leading to its current vacant state. Instead, the Arcade has undergone dramatic peaks and valleys, as it struggled and bounced back several different times over the course of the twentieth century. Despite its architectural splendor and strong support from many in the community, it was never able to sustain prolonged success, but there has always been a dream for it to return to its original form, including today's restoration efforts.

In 1904, the Arcade opened to great fanfare. Local businessmen Eugene Barney (from Barney and Smith Car Company) and Michael Gibbons formulated the initial plans for an arcade in downtown Dayton, and the two recruited noted architect Frank Mills Andrews, who had already designed the NCR factories and the Conover building. Andrews certainly lived up to the lofty expectations. When it was complete, the Arcade was described as "in a class by itself…unlike anything else in the country."[75] Its ornate design included the Flemish-style Third Street façade, which was inspired by a guildhall in Amsterdam. At its opening, the entryway was open to the elements (doors weren't installed until much later), and a long corridor connected shoppers to the opposite entrance on Fourth Street. In the middle was the arcade's centerpiece: a seventy-foot-high glass-domed rotunda that towered above what originally was a two-hundred-stall market house. The

The Dayton Arcade's Flemish-inspired façade on Third Street. *Courtesy of Dayton Metro Library.*

second and third floors of the rotunda overlooked the market, and the abundant light that spilled through the glass dome earned the building the nickname "white palace." Architectural details in the rotunda paid homage to local Ohio produce and game, including "cornucopias full of fruits and vegetables, clusters of oak leaves and acorns, rams' heads and wild turkeys." At the very top of the dome, architect Andrews added pineapples, far from a local fruit but a longstanding symbol of hospitality. From the beginning, the complex was a mixed-use development before that term was even coined, as the arcade also contained offices and apartments, making it "a village within itself in the very heart of the city."[76]

A three-day formal opening ceremony was called the greatest charity event in the history of Dayton due to the massive amount of volunteer labor required to make it happen. In 1904, a *Dayton Journal* reporter described the scene of bustling activity:

> *The scene that meets the eye as one enters on Fourth Street is a bewildering combination of light and colors….You pass up the broad aisle, leaving*

to your right the auditorium, arranged for recitals, and on the left the all white booth where cream candy is being sold on commission....A Japanese tea house is one of the most artistic features of the festival, being in representation of an oriental house with verandas, the rustic work of walls and rails, with the pillars covered with palm fiber, while Japanese lanterns and a great paper dragon add to the picturesque effect....Mahomet's cave received much patronage, the very mystery of the place tending to draw people to see what can be so pleasing. Here one goes through a winding narrow passage, daring to face skeletons, bats and owls, and at last finds himself in a grotto; face to face with the writer of the Koran. The mystery and horror of the long avenue makes the adventurer shiver and when, emerging, he finds himself not ten feet from the entrance, the absurdity of the situation causes considerable merriment.[77]

In a few years' time, the market house vendors began to offer much more than food, including dry goods, jewelry, cigars, haircuts and more. In 1908, the ten-story Commercial Building, the final Arcade building to be built, was erected at the corner of Fourth and Ludlow Streets, connecting to the

The Arcade's grand rotunda once housed a two-hundred-stall market house. *Courtesy of Dayton Metro Library.*

The Commercial Building joined the Dayton Arcade in 1908 at the corner of Fourth and Ludlow. *Courtesy of Dayton Metro Library.*

Ludlow and Fourth Street façades, which are Italian Renaissance Revival style. The Commercial Building was also a prominent part of Dayton's skyline as one of the very few high-rises at the time.

But it took less than a decade for the Arcade to encounter a major disaster: the Great Flood of 1913. As the waters began to rise, some 250 people found themselves trapped in the Arcade. They would not be able to leave for several days, and the floodwaters eventually reached a height of twelve feet. One man, John Breen, was stuck in the neighboring Phillips House hotel with his wife and children when the flood struck. Worried that the flaming logs he saw floating down the street from a burning house might set fire to his hotel, Breen took dramatic action to protect his family. He laid out a board across to the neighboring Gibbons Building and another from there to the Arcade building. He and his family carefully crossed these boards to reach the Arcade, believing it to be a safer and more secure location to wait out the disaster.[78]

After the flood, an inspired cleanup effort helped rebuild a battered Dayton, but even after the water was pumped out and debris removed, the Arcade was far from in the clear. Worry over future flooding prompted many of Dayton's prominent downtown residents to move to the security of streetcar suburbs such as Dayton View that sat on higher elevation. Foot traffic then declined markedly in the Arcade, which led to fewer vendors setting up shop in the marketplace. Nevertheless, many devoted shoppers continued coming, helping to keep the Arcade going.

But soon another monumental threat would emerge to put a damper on the Arcade: war. After the Japanese attack on Pearl Harbor in 1941, many American cities were fearful of the prospect of additional bombings and planned for blackouts, which meant hiding lights to make it difficult for enemy aircraft to plan an attack. In Dayton, the Arcade's dome "looked like a huge round bulls-eye pointing right to the center of the city."[79] Because of these fears, the Arcade's iconic dome was painted over in black, as was the glass above the main walkway. This made the interior of the Arcade dark during the day, and "what was once a place filled with dappled sunshine was transformed into an area that disappeared into darkness. Lights were dropped down to a lower level to help illuminate merchandise better. This caused the dome and its wonderful decorations to almost vanish in the glare of the lights below it. The beauty of the Arcade was all but gone." But again, determined shoppers and brave retail tenants stuck around, and the Arcade made it into the 1950s.

Then the Arcade's next threat made its presence felt. This time it wasn't as drastic as a massive flood or the prospect of world war but rather the proliferation of suburban shopping malls far away from the downtown center. This wasn't an entirely new phenomenon, as corner stores and neighborhood markets serving former downtown residents chipped into the Arcade's market share in the decades following the flood. But this time, it was on another level and proved to be an irreversible trend.

In 1968, the city created a master plan for downtown Dayton in an attempt to strengthen the historic core, of which the Arcade was a significant piece. In 1975, the Arcade was listed in the National Register of Historic Places, making it eligible for federal redevelopment money. That same year, a plan was announced that would later be called Arcade Square, and financing was finally assured in 1979. A total of $15 million was spent on renovations, much of it focusing on the rotunda area as well as the entrances on Third and Fourth Streets. Many businesses left during the year the Arcade was being worked on, although some stayed. May 10, 1980, was the big day, and crowds lined up on Third Street ahead of the grand reopening at 10:00 a.m. Comedian Phyllis Diller performed the ribbon-cutting ceremony. Businesses were signing leases, and it looked like the Arcade was set to enjoy a resurgence. Popular Arcade businesses at that time were varied and loved by their customers. Charley's Raw Bar and Charley's Crab Restaurant gave customers a taste of the East Coast, including Maine lobsters, Dungeness crab, steamers, mussels and more. Lil' Rinaldo's Bake Shoppe offered cookies, breads and pastries and went through two hundred pounds of sugar and six hundred pounds of flour every day.[80] The kosher bakery was a family operation—with its main location at 910 West Fairview Avenue—for over fifty years until its closing in 2015.

A 1981 book titled *Ohio Cities in Trouble* highlighted continuing struggles in the inner city but cited the Arcade as a success story spurring Dayton's renewal and one of the busier places in the city. It also noted that there was a waiting list for the fifty Arcade apartments. But success at the Arcade would not last for long, as there was an almost immediate recession in the early 1980s. The upper-floor apartments were never reopened as promised, and the Arcade went into receivership in 1983. The following year, it was auctioned at a sheriff's sale. The Arcade's new owners knew that business as usual wouldn't work for the Arcade, so they decided to change course. Their idea was to open up a food court in the rotunda basement, which required cutting out the first floor and installing new staircases to access the newly opened-up space, which would be illuminated by light coming through the dome above. The food court was called the Menu, and several restaurants that had been located on the first floor moved down to the new space, to be joined by a few new vendors. The vacated first-floor spaces would then be taken up by retailers.

The Menu opened in August 1986, and although it could seat over two hundred diners, that still was not enough to accommodate the lunch crowds. To avoid the rush, downtown workers could order free delivery to their offices. The Menu was a success, but it still couldn't reverse the losses of the rest of the Arcade. In fact, the retail situation continued to worsen, as only one shop, Lerner's women's apparel, moved into the first-floor spaces that previously housed food vendors. Out of sixty total leasable spaces in the Arcade, only thirty-six were occupied in 1986, and by 1990, that number dropped to twenty-six, nearly the exact same numbers of tenants as during the Arcade's dark days during the Great Depression up until World War II. This time, however, the owners realized that no amount of marketing was going to fill those spaces, and they sent out a letter to tenants announcing the Arcade's closing. Its last day would be March 30, 1991. One tenant, Arcade Seafoods, stayed put after the rest of the Arcade was shuttered, due to the fact that it had a separate entrance on Ludlow Street. It managed to survive there until 2005, at which point it relocated to 111 First Street. The restaurant closed for good in early 2014.

In addition to business decisions made by Arcade owners, larger city initiatives to bolster downtown specifically attempted to generate more customers for the Arcade. In the late 1980s, the city plan called for acquiring and demolishing all buildings on the west side of Main Street between Third and Fourth Streets and replacing them with a twin towers–style office development connected by a walking arcade, which would also connect to the existing arcade on the same block. The buildings in the crosshairs included significant structures such as the Kuhn's building, McRory's store and the Lindsey building. Half of the project was completed, but the city never acquired the rest of the buildings and the south tower was never built. The structure that did go up was known as One Dayton Center, today the Fifth Third Center at 1 South Main.

A series of columns on the Arcade in the *Dayton Daily News* was titled "Frozen in Time." But in reality, over the years, the Arcade was always in flux, reinventing itself and adapting to outside forces that often seemed to be conspiring against its success. As the Arcade occupies such a crucial part of downtown Dayton's identity, almost immediately after its closing, there were efforts to bring it back again. The complex actually did reopen in 1992 and 1993 on a seasonal basis for Holly Days, an event organized by the city with various merchants occupying the space from Thanksgiving to Christmas. As an ideal outcome, it was hoped that Holly Days's success would be enough to jolt the Arcade back to life on a permanent basis, but although it was fairly well attended, this did not happen. In fact, Christmas decorations from 1993 were still up in the rotunda area in 2017.

In 2004, Tony Staub purchased the Arcade from Tom Danis and applied for a permit to demolish it, due to frustration over lack of support for redevelopment and the high costs of maintaining the massive complex. Ideas floated around during these years, including moving the downtown public library or the *Dayton Daily News* into the Arcade, but several major obstacles prevented those plans from going far. Another proposal would have turned the Arcade into a bingo hall, and yet another would have made it an entertainment center with a museum, art gallery and other amusements. In 2007, a group called Friends of the Arcade was formed in an attempt to advocate for and guide redevelopment of the complex. In 2009, Gunther Berg and Wendell Strutz from Wisconsin bought the Arcade for the minimum bid of $615,106.02 in a tax lien sale they saw on eBay. They announced plans to restore and reopen the beloved complex but were unprepared to make any significant headway, and the buildings deteriorated even further under their ownership. In 2013, the windows of the Commercial Building were boarded up due to fears that falling glass would injure passersby. By 2015, Berg and Strutz's LLC owed $435,765.33 in back taxes on the Arcade.

During these years, demolition of the massive complex was again considered, but a feasibility study found that the buildings would cost between $8 million and $13 million to raze. In January 2016, the City of Dayton signed a memorandum of understanding with local developer Miller-Valentine Group and Baltimore-based Cross Street Partners to begin yet another redevelopment effort. Many cautiously hoped that this time the project would actually happen, as the new developers acquired diverse sources of funding, including low-income housing tax credits, state historic tax credits, new market tax credits and more. Tenants are lining up, as the University of Dayton has pledged to be an anchor in the space, and popular downtown businesses, including the Warped Wing brewery, Boston Stoker coffee, Entrepreneurs Center and the Dayton Visual Arts Center, have signed on, too. Plans for the space also include an "innovation hub, connecting the university to other organizations," 130 apartments aimed at artists and other creatives, a kitchen incubator and numerous public event spaces. The developers had planned to announce whether the project was a go by the end of 2017, but that deadline passed without any major news. In March 2018, Miller-Valentine announced it was pulling out of the project, saying it could not move forward at that time. But a few days later, two new partners, Cincinnati-based Model Group and St. Louis–based McCormack Baron Salazar, joined Cross Street Partners, who remain confident in the project's future. The possibility of restoring such an iconic Dayton landmark to a mix of uses reminiscent of its past has tantalized many who eagerly wait for the project to finally move forward.

11

RIKE'S DEPARTMENT STORE

Many cities have an iconic department store closely associated with it—Macy's in New York, Marshall Fields in Chicago, Shillito's in Cincinnati. For Dayton, that store was Rike's. The company dates to 1853 when David L. Rike, who hailed from rural Xenia, founded a dry goods business at 15 and 17 East Third Street with partners Gideon G. Prugh and James J. Joice. The new store's opening announcement in the *Dayton Journal* proclaimed that "every attention will be paid to customers, and no pain spared to show goods," a Rike's mission that would endure for generations. Rike's original partners soon departed, but the operation saw modest growth over the first few decades, as it expanded into larger quarters on East Fifth Street. At times, the firm assumed the names "DL Rike and Company" and "Rike, Hassler and Company" to account for new partners. In 1893, Rike built his first major store at the corner of Main and Fourth Streets. He had expanded beyond just dry goods and had separate departments for "furs, gowns, rugs and menswear," making Rike's a center of fashion within Dayton.[81] As it was directly next to the Reibold Building, the store contributed to "the critical mass of new buildings that would transform the appearance of Dayton's downtown" near the turn of the century.[82] The façade even drew comparisons to Chicago's Columbian Exposition buildings, which took place that same year.[83]

As a businessman, David Rike was said to be progressive in some of his policies, such as hiring a female clerk, which was then contrary to prevailing conservative attitudes. He was also said to be obsessed with order, once knocking over in disgust a display of clothes that he found to be "slightly out of line."[84] But he cultivated an atmosphere that put customer satisfaction above all, which turned shoppers into loyal repeat customers. After David Rike passed away in 1895, his son Frederick took over and led the company to even greater heights. David Rike had married Salome Kumler, daughter of a United Brethren Church bishop, back in 1855, and in 1908, the Rike Dry Goods Company became the Rike-Kumler Company.

Growth was rapid for the company, and in under two decades, it had outgrown its store at Main and Fourth and started to plan a new home. The Rike-Kumler Company built a seven-story building just a few blocks north on Main and Second Streets in 1911, and it opened in 1912. The timing couldn't have been worse, as the flood struck the very next year. Roughly eight feet of water came into the new store, and the entire first floor, including all merchandise, was destroyed. The company was in financial ruins and faced bankruptcy, but Frederick Rike wasn't about to give up. Even though he couldn't get a loan from a local bank, he set an example for his employees

The flagship Rike's department store at Second and Main. It was demolished in 1999. *Courtesy of the Dayton Metro Library.*

by personally shoveling mud out of the wrecked store. Rike still needed financial help in addition to sweat labor, of course, and he was able to get a loan from the Hathaway company in New York City, which loaned to Rike "on the basis of personal reputation rather than faith in the company."[85] Even with the loan, the outlook for Rike's was uncertain, but it recovered quickly and decisively, and Frederick would continue its robust growth.

Rike's was a popular downtown destination at all times of the year, but during the holidays, it became a beloved tradition. Crowds would head downtown for the Rike's Christmas parade, which featured a procession of elaborate floats culminating in Santa's first appearance of the season. He "climbed up a ladder to the top of the overhang located over the display windows [and] down the chimney into Rike's store."[86] Then shoppers would enjoy the store's legendary Christmas displays, which reached a new level at the store in 1945. Two years earlier, in New York City, NCR had put together an exhaustively researched display based on Dickens's *A Christmas Carol* for its corporate offices there. Frederick Rike asked to bring the displays to the Dayton Rike's store, which the company allowed. Over the years, Rike's would put up a variety of displays in its store windows that were enjoyed by masses of holiday shoppers. Another longstanding window display depicted a scene in which "three bears roast marshmallows over a bonfire, jolly skiers head down the mountain, and a rosy-faced trio dressed in snowsuits makes music on violins."[87] For the little ones, Rike's began a holiday tradition unlike any other that let them shop for their families all on their own. The Tike's Shoppe was a holiday shop for kids run by kids featuring gifts priced for a child's budget and older children there to help the younger ones pick out gifts and wrap them. One Rike's Santa, Al Cole, recalls a year in the 1960s when he talked to 2,500 children in one day, while four other Santas were working at the same time.[88]

Rike's, of course, wasn't the only game in town during the glory days of downtown retail, and another big player in Dayton retail was Elder-Beerman, whose downtown store was in the Reibold Building, for a period of time right next to Rike's. Other downtown Dayton stores included Adler & Child's, the Metropolitan, Donenfeld's and others.

As the years passed, the downtown Rike's store significantly expanded, topping out at eleven stories with a separate annex as an addition. In 1947, the third Rike generation took the helm when Frederick died and his son, also named David, took over, never wavering from the company's characteristic focus on customer service. In 1953, Rike's celebrated one hundred years in business in Dayton with a large celebration, at a time when it had expanded to 504,000 total square feet and was the fourth-largest employer in the city. The company also maintained offices nationally and internationally, including in New York City, London and Yokohama, Japan. The downtown Dayton store featured much more than shopping, including a restaurant on the fifth floor, a radio station, a beauty parlor and even an in-store hospital. One shopper referred to it as a "self-contained little city," because everything you needed was available on one of its floors.

But Rike's faced a decision as retail began to significantly shift to the booming suburbs in the 1950s. Initially, it refused to change strategy but soon caved to the pressure and opened stores in Dayton's suburbs, with the first one located at Dorothy Lane and Woodman in Kettering in 1961. Over the next decade, it would establish stores at Salem Mall in Trotwood (1963) and also one at Upper Valley Mall in Springfield (1971). But at the same time, it made a significant bet on downtown Dayton retail by reinvesting in its flagship location. It was a bet that paid off for a while but eventually would prove untenable given Dayton's larger decline.

Downsizing began in 1980, when Rike's vacated the seventh, eighth and ninth floors, and two years later, it closed the sixth floor as well. Around this time, Rike's, which was now part of the Federated Department Stores

The Schuster Center for the Performing Arts and an accompanying condo tower have replaced Rike's. *Author photo.*

chain, merged with Shillito's, Cincinnati's first department store, and became Shillito-Rike's. The latter part of the 1980s saw more layoffs and closures to the auto service center, the bakery and the parking garage at Main Street and Monument Avenue. The store was renamed again to Lazarus, and a new company bought the Federated chain, which led to even further cutbacks. In 1988, one hundred workers were laid off, but the following year, Lazarus president Mark Cohen proclaimed that the downtown store would remain open. The vote of confidence, however, would be short-lived. Federated filed for Chapter 11 bankruptcy, and when it restructured as a public company, it quickly closed forty of its stores. On January 31, 1992, the company announced that the downtown Dayton store would shut its doors for good. The building survived until 1999, and when it was slated to be demolished, the *Dayton Daily News* asked readers to send in their memories of Rike's. The newspaper was overwhelmed by the many hundreds of letters that flowed in, ranging from handwritten notes to multipage tributes printed on company letterhead. The building's demolition made way for the Schuster Center for the Performing Arts, which was completed in 2003. This new complex is the home of the Dayton Philharmonic, Dayton Ballet and Dayton Opera, which bring dozens of world-class performances each year to Dayton's Main Street. And perhaps most importantly, the center maintains the tradition of the Rike's Christmas displays, setting them up each year in the windows of the lobby.

PART IV

EARLY SKYSCRAPERS

M ain Street in downtown Dayton was home to a number of impressive early skyscrapers, including the Callahan Building, the Reibold Building and the United Brethren Building (Centre City Building), all of which were added to over time. Together, they helped Dayton become a new class of city—one that towered high into the sky and literally elevated public perception of the downtown area as a dynamic center of commerce. The fates of these buildings have diverged significantly in the decades since. The Callahan is long gone, and the Reibold was remodeled and is well occupied by county offices. The Centre City Building stands vacant but awaits a chance at a new life.

Dayton's status as an industrial powerhouse was evident in its growing skyline. *Courtesy of Dayton Metro Library.*

CALLAHAN BUILDING

Considered Dayton's first skyscraper, the Callahan Building was seven stories high—including a clock tower and steeply pitched roof—when it was built in 1892. Its location on the prominent northeast corner of Third and Main Streets had previously been occupied by a small log cabin Presbyterian church built in 1804, as well as by Dayton's first cemetery.[89] The building was the creation of W.P. Callahan, an Irish immigrant who came to Dayton in 1853 and worked as a cabinetmaker and pattern shop foreman before becoming a prominent businessman and eventually the president of City National Bank.[90]

Paul Laurence Dunbar, an influential African American poet from Dayton, had a job as an elevator operator in the Callahan Building when he was starting to work on his writing craft. He earned four dollars a week for his labor, but the influence on his future career may have been the bigger reward, as explained in a *Dayton Daily News* article:

> *Working in the hub of Dayton's commercial district exposed Dunbar to a wealth of different accents and dialects that he was able to work into his writing. And the poet, who was about 20 at the time, had enough down time between elevator passengers to work on what would become his first published volume of poetry,* Oak and Ivy.[91]

By 1914, the Callahan Building had a variety of tenants, including multiple life insurance companies, several attorneys, a dry cleaner, a dentist

The original Callahan Building, Dayton's first true skyscraper, was erected at the busy corner of Third and Main in 1892. *Courtesy of Dayton Metro Library.*

and McBride's Detective Agency, the oldest detective agency in Dayton. In 1920, the top two floors were removed, replaced by seven new floors and topped by a refurbished clock. The new Callahan Building had some quirks; it was described in one architectural history as featuring a "complex dormered roof featuring a corner tower, an appendage more European than American, more medieval than modern," an unusual style for the time.[92] The clock was missing from the building for nearly a year, but it was finally reinstalled in April 1921 by City National Bank, which often advertised itself as the "bank under the clock." Bank president H.H. Darst thought the children of Dayton should get an early start on building the habit of saving money. He presented bankbooks to all students in Dayton Public Schools, and each student made a deposit every Tuesday morning that ended up in the vaults of the Callahan Building. Teacher Lucia May Wiant suggested that Darst allow two students, one boy and one girl, to restart the iconic clock after its repairs. A poetry-memorizing contest was used to select the lucky pupils, and the final rounds were held at Steele High School, where attendees included Darst and Dayton mayor J.M. Switzer. Wiant, however, found it too difficult to select the winners, so she picked two names out of a hat instead.[93] The clock was illuminated at night by 784 powerful lamps, 464 of which were on the clock face.[94] It became an important symbol associated with downtown Dayton.

In 1955, the building got a new name when it was bought by Gem City and became the Gem City Savings Building. The Callahan Building and surrounding buildings were demolished in July 1978 to make way for the I.M. Pei–designed Gem City Plaza, now the National City Center. Because the iconic clock wasn't going to fit in with the modernist architectural theme, many Daytonians were worried that the most famous clock in the city's history would be destroyed along with one of its prominent early buildings. But E.R. Strasser of Reynolds and Reynolds stepped in, and the clock moved to the company's Germantown Street complex near I-75. But that structure, too, would later see its days numbered, and it was slated to be demolished in 2006. Once again, the clock's fate was uncertain. A developer pledged to move it to a new building at the corner of Third and Jefferson, but that promise was left unfulfilled. Instead, the clock was moved to Carillon Park, where it still resides today.[95] One man, Danny Worthington, helped lower the iconic clock off the Callahan Building in 1978 and assisted in its removal from the Reynolds and Reynolds building twenty-eight years later.[96] It was recently announced that the clock will soon rise high in the air once again, as an upcoming Carillon Park expansion will include a one-hundred-foot-tall tower with the clock at the top.

REIBOLD BUILDING

The Reibold Building became Dayton's tallest structure when it was constructed in 1896, and it was added to twice more in the next twenty years. Its first tenant was the Elder Johnson department store, one of dozens of dry goods stores found around Dayton at the time. Once it moved from its first location at 114–16 East Third Street to the new Reibold Building, the store quickly expanded from two floors to five, and when the first addition was completed in 1905, Elder Johnson took up space there as well, due to its steady growth. The third and final addition to the Reibold Building was the annex built in 1914 that gave the building a total of just over 349,000 square feet. The building was a crowning achievement for businessman Louis N. Reibold, and both Charles Insco Williams and prominent firm Peters, Burns and Pretzinger were credited as architects. It was considered by many to be the most beautiful building in Dayton at the time, with architectural details that included a terra-cotta exterior, six-foot-high Italian marble wainscoting, Honduran mahogany finishes and maple floors.[97]

The Reibolds had strict guidelines for their tenants, as described in one of their brochures: "As an example, every doctor and dentist in the Reibold Building is strictly ethical. No quacks or advertisers allowed. No individual or corporation of doubtful reputation will be admitted. Being a tenant of the Reibold Building is a boost to your prestige."[98] Offices even boasted "ornate doorknobs emblazoned with a large 'R'."[99]

According to Emporis, "The Otis Elevator Company installed four escalators here in 1934, the first ones in Dayton. These escalators are still

The Reibold Building, Dayton's tallest when it was built, with its first addition (*left*). To the right is the location Rike's occupied from 1893 to 1912. *Courtesy of Dayton Metro Library.*

operational and are, with escalators in Connecticut and at the Smithsonian, the only examples surviving from that era."[100]

In 1972, the 350,000-square-foot Reibold Building was bought by Montgomery County for just $860,000, a bargain price due to the migration of most businesses to the suburbs around this time. At first, the plan was to chop off the upper six floors to save money on maintenance, but fortunately, this was not executed. The building suffered architecturally in the following years, as explained in a *Dayton Daily News* article:

> *In July 1987, this column criticized the neglect of maintenance that had led to deterioration of the terra cotta ornament and cornice on the facade. The county already had spent $6 million to provide human services and archive offices. A brutal 1981 rehab added tacky Las Vegas canopies, a barren covered walkway around two sides and big, brazen glass panels over the battered facade. More of the fabric was lost in a 1988 rehab, partly for safety reasons.[101]*

In 1997, the building lost half of its workers when the Job Opportunity Center moved its four hundred employees to a new location on Edwin C. Moses Boulevard. For a while, the future of the building was up in the air, but the county soon transferred new offices into the space.

Fortunately, an extensive $12 million renovation begun that same year and finished four years later helped bring the building back to productive office use. In 2001, construction began on a $7 million eight-story parking garage for county employees. Today, the county occupies the Reibold Building for its Combined Health District, the Support and Enforcement Agency of Job and Family Services Department, Adult Probation, County Prosecutor, Juvenile Court and the County Archive and Records Center.

UNITED BRETHREN BUILDING

Today's Centre City Building was originally the home of the United Brethren Publishing House. Like the Reibold, it was built in three phases, the first of which was a fourteen-story structure that took the honor of tallest building in Dayton away from the Reibold in 1904. A few years later, an addition was made on the north side, and in 1924, the tower was completed, making the United Brethren Building twenty-one stories. It remained the tallest building in Dayton until 1931, when the Liberty Tower (originally the Mutual Home Savings Association building) was erected at 120 West Second Street.

The motivation for the United Brethren Building came from William R. Funk, publishing agent for United Brethren, which was then a very important publishing house. United Brethren Publishing House was founded in 1834 in Circleville, Ohio, and moved to Dayton the following year, publishing a wide variety of religious and devotional books and periodicals, including *Our Bible Lesson Quarterly* and *Lessons for the Little Ones*.[102] The company bought the land at the northeast corner of Fourth and Main and, in 1854, built a four-story building at that corner. But Funk had much larger ambitions.

He "dreamed of building an office tower whose profits would provide adequate pensions for retired ministers and their families."[103] Architect Charles Herby of Dayton designed the new UB Building, and it was built by the FA Requarth Company, which later became a lumber company and is still located in downtown Dayton near the ballpark on Monument Avenue. The structure represents the Chicago Commercial style and is the only

Left: The first phase of the United Brethren Building was built in 1904, replacing the four-story building that had been built at the corner of Main and Fourth in 1853. *Courtesy of Dayton Metro Library.*

Right: One of the tallest reinforced-concrete buildings in the world when its final phase was complete, what is today called the Centre City Building awaits new life. *Courtesy of Dayton Metro Library.*

example of such a skyscraper in Dayton. When it was completed, it was said to be the tallest reinforced-concrete building in the world.

The building also had connections to the Wright family. Milton Wright was a minister for the Church of the United Brethren, and when he was elected editor of the church's newspaper, the *Religious Telescope*, he moved his family to Dayton because it was the location of the publishing office. His sons, Orville and Wilbur, later had an office in the building. For a little over a year in 1910–11, the Wright Company Exhibition Department took up office space in room 1310, during a time when the brothers thought that focusing on flying demonstrations would bring better business than actually producing airplanes.[104] The building was also known for retail, as a longtime tenant of the building was the Adler and Child's Department Store, which closed in 1950.

United Brethren sold the building in 1952 due to financial struggles, and it was purchased by the Knott Hotel group from New York. In 1975, the Vontz Realty Company bought the building, and Albert and Essie Vontz converted the top floor into a penthouse apartment, where they lived for many years, long before downtown lofts became common in Dayton. Retail remained at the ground levels, but tenants slowly left during the 2000s, and soon the building was completely vacant.

Since then, the building has changed hands several times and various redevelopment projects proposed, but developers have been unable to get them off the ground even after winning state historic tax credits. The most recent proposal won $5 million in tax credits, but remaining gaps in financing and the sheer size of the building make it a difficult task.

Both the Centre City and the Reibold Buildings, the two of this trio that survive, face the cleared-out Dave Hall Plaza (where the State Theater once stood), which is being transformed into the Levitt Pavilion, sponsored by a foundation that will provide fifty free downtown concerts and likely inject some life into a now sleepy part of downtown Dayton.

PART V

RECREATION/EDUCATION

15

LAKESIDE PARK

The Dayton VA Medical Center and adjacent National Cemetery are fixtures of Dayton's far west side, as they have been for over 150 years. But today there's little trace of their lost neighbor: a major amusement park that was the site of innovative rides and attractions over the years.

The precursor to today's Department of Veterans Affairs was called the National Home for Disabled Volunteer Soldiers, authorized by Congress in 1866. Three branches were initially established, and Dayton was given the Central Branch, which also served as the administrative center. The idyllic pastoral setting and beautifully landscaped grounds became a popular attraction for over 350,000 visitors a year in addition to its resident veterans, and it was a place where "many people turned for amusement—whether it be an entertaining play, an exhilarating parade, celebration of a holiday, or just a quiet stroll through the beautiful grounds of the Home." Special events included a balloon ascent on August 12, 1880, during which Professor James Allen and his son—in front of a crowd of ten thousand—floated up in the air in a large balloon that blew south and eventually landed on a farm four miles west of Middletown.[105]

In 1890, Moses More (or James Kirk or E.J. Laterbach; little is known about the original owner) took advantage of the Home's popularity by setting up a new venture right next door. A forty-foot-high cyclorama depicting the Battle of Gettysburg had already been built as an attraction in 1887, and this was expanded in the area into a complete amusement park called Dahomey Amusement Park, although everyone came to call it Lakeside.

A popular water ride at Lakeside called Shooting the Chutes involved riders hurtling down toward the water in a flat-bottomed boat, which skittered across the water's surface until it slowed down. *Courtesy of Dayton Metro Library.*

A 1905 advertisement for Lakeside Park praised its setting and quality, describing it as "where all the summer sports and amusements of the seaside can be seen…where woodland, grotos [*sic*], lakes and flowing fountains, and where the blossoms of the world mingle their fragrance in one solid sheet… [and] where you can see variety and make your outing one of pleasure, education and pleasant memory."[106] The same ad boldly declared it "without a parallel in America, and perhaps the world."

The park's roller-skating rink, where skaters circled to the sounds of a full military band, was called the best in the state in 1909. The park was purchased by Lakeside Park Co. Inc. in 1913, and in 1916, the company installed a new rococo carousel built by the Philadelphia Toboggan Company with "gilded hand-carved horses and wooden cherubs clutching mandolins."[107]

Lakeside Park would go on to feature many more cutting-edge rides and attractions over the ensuing decades, many of which were built practically next door on South Hatfield Street. The National Amusement Company, founded in 1920 by Aural Vaszin, was one of the first companies to manufacture roller coasters, and Vaszin had the benefit of a natural testing ground for his innovations at Lakeside.

Many of Lakeside's rides were unique and unusual, including the Derby Racer wooden roller coaster, the Flying Turns ride ("where single cars sped down a trough instead of a track") and the Wildcat roller coaster.[108] In those days, one could take a streetcar from downtown and spend the whole day enjoying the rides, penny arcade, Hilarity Hall funhouse and myriad other attractions.

But it wasn't always all fun and games at Lakeside. A racial disturbance broke out in 1919 due to resentment boiling over from discriminatory policies at the park. In general, African Americans were allowed, but they were not permitted to enter the dance pavilion and had to stick to certain horses on the carousel. According to an account by E.T. Banks, a friend of Paul Laurence Dunbar, these restrictions "had laid the foundation for attacks against black people," one of which occurred on July 20, 1919, after whites had ordered blacks out of the concession area and theater and began to fight. The conflict also spilled onto the streetcars heading back to town afterward, with groups reportedly stopping certain cars and beating black riders.[109] But despite this disturbance, Banks urged blacks to continue to go to Lakeside without fear, for "fear enslaves body and soul."[110]

The Great Depression forced many amusement parks to close, but Lakeside survived, as it was annexed by the City of Dayton in 1930 and continued chugging along. In this heyday of general amusement parks for all

Many recreational activities awaited at Lakeside Park. *Courtesy of Dayton Metro Library.*

ages, Dayton boasted many more than just Lakeside. There was also White City Amusement Park near Helena Street, which was destroyed in the flood after only three years of operation. The site, however, was quickly turned into Island Park, which still exists today as a public park in the Five Rivers Metroparks system. There was also Forest Park on North Main Street near Needmore Road, today the site of a shopping center. And popular Fairview Park, also just off North Main, lasted from 1887 to 1915 on the site of today's E.J. Brown School.

All of these parks eventually met their end, and around 1950, Lakeside Park's decline had started to accelerate. It didn't help that the president and general manager of Lakeside, Gerald Niermann, pleaded guilty to tax evasion in 1951 and was jailed for six months. And the 1950s and early 1960s also saw a series of major accidents at the park. In 1953, a thirteen-year-old boy was injured on a ride and eventually won $22,500 in damages from a federal court jury. In 1960, eight students from Fairview High School who were at the park for a prom outing were ejected from the Merry Mix-Up ride and suffered injuries. Finally, in 1962, a nineteen-year-old man died after falling off a roller coaster. Alongside these major accidents, financial woes continued to mount for Lakeside. The park was shut down in 1964 and would remain closed for the next three years, at which point the Dayton Municipal Court auctioned off all but eight rides and most of the rest of the park equipment.

The last remnants of the park, including the Lakeview Palladium dance hall, which was a 1968 remodel of the park's previous ballroom, were demolished in 1993 for the expansion of I-35. The lake suffered extreme neglect in the following years, as the highway crosses directly over it, and those who wished to go fishing had to climb over a guardrail to do so. But in the summer of 2017, groups of volunteers, many living in the surrounding neighborhoods, organized clean-ups for the lake and its surroundings. Other organizations, including the Garden Club of Dayton, CityWide development and local union groups, have assisted the neighborhood volunteers, and long-term plans include more than just cleaning. The groups envision installing a floating fishing pier as well as creating walking paths, adding more parking and improving signage and lighting around the park. There will never again be roller coasters on the grounds of Lakeside Park, but supporters hope it soon will be an area where residents of Dayton's West Side Pineview neighborhood can once again go to enjoy spending a day outdoors in a beautiful setting.

TRIANGLE PARK
(DAYTON TRIANGLES)

The major role of Canton, Ohio, in the development of football is widely known: it's where the first professional league was conceived, as well as the site of the current Pro Football Hall of Fame. And Cleveland and Cincinnati, of course, today have NFL teams embroiled in a cross-state rivalry. But Dayton's place in football history flies much more under the radar. Many have forgotten that the Gem City was significantly involved in the establishment of what is today the NFL and that the burgeoning league's first game was played right here in Dayton. Today, the NFL does not trace any current franchise back to Dayton's original team: the Triangles. Given the history, however, perhaps it should.

The story of the Triangles starts in 1912, one mile south of downtown at St. Mary's College, today the University of Dayton. A group of recently graduated basketball players formed a club basketball team called the St. Mary's Cadets, which also included college students as well as other players from around Dayton. Although the team enjoyed a great deal of success—in particular, winning a national championship by defeating the Buffalo Germans, widely considered the best team in the country—the players gradually shifted their focus to the gridiron.

Amateur and semipro football teams were already widespread in the Dayton area, as by 1910, teams calling themselves the Wolverines, Miamis, McKinleys, Westwoods, Oxfords, Republics and Nationals played at various parks around the city.[111] This was an era in which many semipro football players worked their factory jobs during the day, practiced in the evening and then played in games on the weekend, earning themselves some extra money.

The former St. Mary's players formed a football team in 1913 and retained the Cadets name. The team went an undefeated 7-0 during its first season and won two city championships before changing its name to the Dayton Gym-Cadets. It was sponsored by the athletic club of that name, which was located on Wayne Avenue.

But the influence of major Dayton industrialists took the team to the next level. Delco, run by Edward Deeds and Charles Kettering, started organizing recreational football for its workers in 1916. The bulk of the new team was made up of Cadets players, and the new coach was Nelson (Bud) Talbott, who lived in Oakwood and had recently been named an All-American while playing football at Yale. Assisting Talbott in organizing the squad was Carl (Scummy) Storck, a Cadets player and "one of the first men in America to envision a future professional league,"[112] which would become significant a few years later.

The new team's name, the Dayton Triangles, came from the "triangle" of three downtown factories: Delco, Delco Light and Dayton Metal Products. The Triangles' first game couldn't have gone better, as the team defeated the Cincinnati Northerns by a score of 72–0. The team would soon get a new field that fit its name perfectly when Deeds and Kettering bought a large triangular-shaped piece of land north of downtown for their workers to use for sport and recreation.

In August and September 1920, team representatives met in the Canton, Ohio Hubmobile showroom of Ralph Hay, owner of the Canton Bulldogs, to discuss forming the league that would become the NFL. The Triangles were represented by Storck and became a founding member of the fledgling league. Other franchises included the Akron Pros, Canton Bulldogs, Cleveland Indians, Decatur Staleys, Hammond Pros, Massillon Tigers, Muncie Flyers, Racine Cardinals, Rochester Jeffersons and Rock Island Independents. At its founding, the league was called the American Professional Football Association (APFA).

The Triangles hosted the Columbus Panhandles in the inaugural league game the following month, on October 3, 1920, and Dayton emerged victorious in a 14–0 shutout behind scores from running back Louis Partlow, who scored the league's first touchdown, and Francis Bacon. Partlow was known to employ an interesting method of practice in which he ran "through heavily wooded country along the Miami River near his home in West Carrollton. He would run close to the trees, as if picking a

In the 1920 season, the Dayton Triangles went 5-2-2. *Public domain.*

hole, and occasionally run full tilt into one of them to toughen up his shoulder for blocking."[113]

That season, the Triangles finished a highly respectable 5-2-2. The only team it lost to was Akron, which ended up winning the league championship with a victory over the Decatur Staleys. Two years later, the Staleys would adopt a more recognizable name: the Chicago Bears.

But times would get much tougher for the Triangles in the following years, and it would never again achieve a record as good as in that inaugural season. In 1921, the team went 4-4-1 and in 1922, the year the league officially adopted the National Football League name, it finished 4-3-1. This would prove to be its final winning season. Over the following seven years, the Triangles would win only five games total, and after back-to-back winless seasons in 1928 and 1929, the writing was on the wall. Because of this lack of success, the team's folding "was not widely mourned in Dayton."[114]

Carl Storck, who served as head coach of the Triangles from 1922 to 1926, sold the team in 1930 to Prohibition bootlegger "Big Bill" Dwyer, who brought the team to Brooklyn and gave it the same name as the borough's baseball team, the Dodgers. Both Brooklyn teams played their home games at Ebbets Field, and the NFL Dodgers survived into the 1940s. In 1945, it merged with the Boston Yanks, which subsequently moved back to New York to become the Bulldogs and then the Yanks again. In 1951, the owner sold the franchise back to the NFL, and its new owner took the team to Dallas and named it the Dallas Texans. The Texans were sold back to the league in the middle of the 1952 season, and the following season, what remained of the organization was given to the new Baltimore expansion team, which would be named the Colts. The Colts moved to Indianapolis in 1984, capping an indirect lineage from the Triangles to a current NFL team. The NFL doesn't officially recognize the Brooklyn Dodgers as the same franchise as the Colts, however, let alone the Triangles. As for Storck, he became treasurer of the NFL from 1921 to 1939 and league president from 1939 to 1941.

These days, baseball fans pack the Single A Dayton Dragons' Fifth Third Field on the edge of downtown—even setting a record for most consecutive sellouts by any professional team in 2011—but the prospect of a major professional league team in Dayton seems improbable. But for a short period in the 1920s, the Triangles were an instrumental part of the launch of professional football and likely deserve more recognition for their role.

Triangle Park had a capacity of five thousand spectators in its heyday, but the original field and grandstands are long gone. Later, the Howell Field baseball diamond was built on the site, and it, too, has a proud history, including when Pete Rose played there frequently for a Dayton amateur league in 1960. The original Triangles' locker room, however, remained in the parking lot next to Howell Field and was still being used for storage of garden tools in 2012, when it was moved to Carillon Park.

A historical marker denotes the spot in Triangle Park where Dayton defeated the Columbus Panhandles in the NFL's first game. *Author photo.*

In April 2005, the Ohio Historical Society unveiled a new historic marker commemorating the site. The current Triangle Park also features a park pavilion, picnic tables and extensive recreational areas, but aside from the easy-to-miss plaque, nothing else suggests that the nondescript area was once the site of the NFL's first game.

PUBLIC LIBRARY

Dayton's most iconic library was a beautiful French Gothic Romanesque design built on Cooper Park, the city's oldest green space, near the center of downtown. But before that building was constructed, a public library existed for decades in more makeshift locations around town.

Dayton was the first city in Ohio to incorporate a public library, and it did so in 1805, its first year of official existence. Benjamin Van Cleve, a pioneer settler of Dayton, served as the first librarian of what was then called the Social Library Society. During its early years, the library's books were kept in Van Cleve's own cabin on First and St. Clair, a dwelling that also functioned as Dayton's post office. In these years, the library was described as "two well-filled bookcases," but in 1835, the administrators sold the books at auction, which put an end to Dayton's library.[115]

But the concept would resurface again in 1846 when a group of Daytonians proposed a public library that would serve a greater number of citizens. A public meeting was held at city hall on December 29, 1846, when the newly formed Dayton Library Association adopted its constitution. Although it was a public library, membership wasn't free in those days, and dues were three dollars for an annual membership, thirty dollars for a lifetime membership or fifty dollars for membership in perpetuity. Minors, however, could use the library free of charge as long as they abided by the rules set by the board of directors, which at that time featured prominent Daytonians, including Robert Steele, Ebenezer Thresher and Daniel Beckel.

The first location was the Steele Building, where the library was open on Fridays from 3:00 p.m. to 6:00 p.m. and 7:00 p.m. to 10:00 p.m. In 1853, the library moved to the new Phillips Building at the corner of Second and Main Streets. During this era, libraries looked much different from the open, welcoming institutions we think of today. When located on the second floor of the Phillips Building, although the library rooms were elegant—with oak furniture, bronze pilasters and two large Corinthian columns—the books "were behind wire screens like burglar-proof basement windows," and patrons were prohibited from handling them at all times.[116]

By the late 1850s, the library was struggling mightily, due to both declining budgets and competition from a second library. In 1855, the free Public School Library was established in Dayton after a state law was passed allocating funds for school libraries. In Dayton, the school board chose to establish a central library rather than set up smaller collections at each district school, and it was located in the United Brethren Building. As this new institution was centralized and open to all and benefited from outside funding, it greatly affected the existing public library. The library association sought to combine the two libraries, and this was achieved in 1860, the same year the first full-time librarian was hired. By 1867, the library collection had exceeded ten thousand volumes, and it would again be on the move. This time, it moved into the City Building in the Central Market House, where it took a space on the second floor. In 1877, that building was demolished and a new city building constructed on the same site, with the library occupying rooms "fitted with heavily moulded black walnut book-cases arranged in alcoves with a gallery on three sides and the librarian's desk in the center." There was "dignity in all the appointments and the books" due to the longtime collecting habits of Robert W. Steele, but there was no library catalogue and the concept of reference service still did not exist.

Starting in the 1870s, the library committee had begun looking to put an end to its moving and build a permanent home. Its spaces were becoming too crowded, and fireproof construction was greatly desired. A leading candidate for a new building location was Cooper Park, left as public green space in Daniel Cooper's original 1803 Dayton plat. The park occupied a square block right in the heart of downtown, bounded by Second, St. Clair and Third Streets. There was some concern over using dedicated parkland for another purpose, however, as the deed for the square stated it be "enclosed, planted with trees, and forever kept as a walk for the citizens of Dayton and its visitors."[117] But it turned out that the city had bought out the interests of Cooper's heirs long ago, and in 1887, part of Cooper Park was set aside for the library to construct its new facility.

The 1888 building was widely considered the "largest and best building in the state of Ohio devoted exclusively to library purposes."[118] A dedication given during an opening gala event attended by over seven hundred described the building's style as "a free treatment of the Southern French Gothic, or Romanesque, built of Dayton limestone, laid in random range work, with Marquette red sandstone trimmings freely used, giving it a very rich contrast, assisted largely by red slate for the roof."[119] To design the interior, officials had solicited the recommendation of prominent librarian William Frederick Poole, who had worked in Chicago and Boston and in addition had led the Cincinnati Public Library to be the first in the country to (controversially) open on Sundays.

Library trustees had long envisioned establishing a museum of natural history to complement the public library, and in 1893, they set up such

The old public library. The William McKinley statue still stands in another part of Cooper Park. *Courtesy of Dayton Metro Library.*

a museum on the library's second floor, making it the first library in the state with a museum. It remained there until 1921, when the museum was moved to the Steele Building on Second and Ludlow due to overcrowding at the main library. The museum still exists, as it later became the Dayton Museum of Natural History in 1952. In the 1990s, its board merged with a group attempting to establish a children's museum. That merger created the Dayton Museum of Discovery, which is today called the Boonshoft Museum of Discovery and is located north of downtown.

In 1895, traveling libraries that went to Dayton public school classrooms were established, and a separate School Department Library opened in the library's basement to be used by local schoolchildren, who could take out a book a week. Soon, a system of neighborhood branch libraries was needed to supplement the central library, and in 1911, the library won Carnegie funds to erect one library on the east side of town and one on the west side. They both opened in 1914. The east branch, at 2160 East Fifth Street, still stands and is today used by the St. Mary Development Corporation, but the west side library burned in 1979 and was torn down. Branch collections housed in Dayton schools came next, and then the first non-Carnegie freestanding branch to be built was the Electra C. Doren branch in North Dayton on Troy Street, which is the oldest Dayton library still in service today. It was named for the longtime Dayton librarian who, in the 1890s, a time when library service was quickly evolving, established a library training school at the main library—only two library schools existed in the country at the time.[120] She also opened the stacks up to library patrons for the first time. In 1923, the Book Wagon program (which later became the Bookmobile) was launched, originally serving twenty-six stations throughout Dayton.

During the Great Depression, the Dayton library became an even more popular destination for citizens seeking everything from leisure reading as an escape from their predicaments to materials to help train for new jobs. Library staff worked for months without pay in order to stay open and meet the needs of the community during a trying time.[121]

In 1945, the library board hired a consultant to explore the possibility of a new central library "and of any extension or remodeling of the present branch provisions" for the library system. A bond issue was presented that same year, but it narrowly lost out. But the push for a new building remained strong, and about a decade later, it was given the green light. In 1962, the grand public library was demolished for a new library that was located next door, with frontage on Third Street. Books were moved by a conveyor belt during the transition. During the latter half of the twentieth century, which

Today's modern library opened in 2017. *Author photo.*

One of the few buildings to remain from the canal days, the longtime Hauer Music building (*right*) is today the public library operations center. *Courtesy of Dayton Metro Library.*

saw many major technological advancements, Dayton's library kept pace, opening an audiovisual department in 1973, debuting its first computers in 1984, replacing the card catalogue with public computer terminals in 1991 and providing internet access to the public in 1996.[122] But the modernist design of the new library was soon considered drab and uninspired, and it, too, eventually became outdated and too small.

Today, a new state-of-the art library, aided by a $187 million bond issue passed in 2012, stands on the site. The 1962 building was stripped down to its structural core and then given a massive expansion to 120,000 total square feet, a massive increase from what had originally been 30,000. The addition on the northwest corner of Third Street and Patterson Boulevard is three stories and is full of windows that look out on downtown Dayton and Webster Station. The new library officially opened to the public on August 5, 2017, and features numerous community rooms, 135 new computers, a theater, a performance space with a capacity of 299 people, an underground parking garage and art by local artists on the walls.

But the new library does continue to maintain some connection to the old buildings that once lined the canal that is today Patterson Boulevard. The library moved its operations center to the former Hauer Music building, built in 1888 to house the Sachs-Pruden Ale Company brewery and later a warehouse for the Lowe Brothers Paint Company. It is located just a block down Patterson from the library's public facility.

STEELE HIGH SCHOOL

A Romanesque Revival wood structure constructed in 1894 on Monument Avenue and Main Street near the Great Miami River, Steele High School was Dayton's only high school until 1906. Alter Rafner, a member of the class of 1938, once described the grand building that was Steele: "The school's architecture was imported from Europe, and when completed looked like a castle. It was a towered and turreted gem of a building. The school symbol was a lion. The bronze lion sculpture graced the front cement steps leading from the pavement to the front door."[123]

Steele cost $325,000 to build, which was an extremely large sum at the time and one that left over little for decoration of the school grounds or the interior. Because of this, Steele students and teachers formed the Decorative Art Association, whose members paid a membership fee of five cents per month, which was pooled together to purchase artwork. This group purchased hundreds of pieces of art in the following years, including a small lion sculpture that unfortunately deteriorated. Steele students and faculty liked the lion, so they attempted to replace it with a much more impressive version. The new lion was created by prominent sculptor Anna Hyatt Huntington, who took inspiration from a lion at the Bronx Zoo in New York City. The project was aided financially by the school's own students, who helped raise over $300, mostly in nickels.[124] It took ten years to raise enough money to create the statue, but it would be well worth the wait. Once work began, Hyatt even traveled to Naples, Italy, in 1907 to supervise the bronze casting of the sculpture. An unveiling ceremony was held at Steele on December 11, 1908, which included a speech by Hyatt and a performance by the Steele High School band. The lion, dubbed Leo, also earned adoration far beyond the limits of Dayton, as a Paris journal called it "the finest representation of the American movement to place art in the schools in order to elevate public taste."[125]

For many years, Steele had a prominent neighbor: Newcom Tavern, the oldest surviving structure in Dayton, built in 1796. That building was moved in the late 1800s from its original location at Main and Water Streets (now Monument Avenue) to a site on the river right next to Steele at Van Cleve Park, today part of Riverscape Metropark. In 1965, Newcom Tavern moved again, to Carillon Historical Park, where it still is today.

The school was named for longtime school board president and writer Robert W. Steele, whose longtime residence is today the Dayton Woman's Club. Steele High School's first principal was Captain Charles Stivers, who during the Civil War fought in the Battle of Fredericksburg and served as a battalion commander at the Battles of Rouse's Point and Skipper's Gap. After recovering from an injury sustained during battle, he came to Dayton in 1865 to lead the Western Military Academy. Once he retired from the military, Stivers became a teacher in the Dayton public schools, and in 1872, he was named principal of Central High School on Fourth and Wilkinson Streets, which was then Dayton's only high school. Notable pupils during his

Leo the Lion survived Steele's demolition and was moved to the Dayton Art Institute. *Courtesy of Dayton Metro Library.*

Steele High School was razed in 1955, but Newcom Tavern (*left*), the oldest surviving structure in Dayton, originally built in 1796, now stands in Carillon Historical Park. *Courtesy of Dayton Metro Library.*

time at Central included Orville Wright and Paul Laurence Dunbar, who were members of the same class.

Stivers served as principal at Central for over two decades, and he played a major role in the planning of a grand new high school that would be Steele. During that time there was "grave doubt" among some that Dayton needed a new and expensive high school, but Stivers "saw into the future" and "urged the High School question at all times"[126] until the new building was finally constructed. He oversaw the transition to the new building, and then, once his mission was accomplished, he resigned his position as principal. (He would be honored later on when Dayton's second high school was renamed for him in the 1920s.) Central High was demolished in 1893, and a new district school was built in its place.

Wilbur and Orville Wright's sister Katherine taught Latin at Steele for a decade around the turn of the twentieth century. Another of Steele's many notable teachers was Eleanor G. Brown, the first blind person to receive a doctorate from Columbia University. Born in 1888 in Osborn (today

Steele High School was badly damaged during the March 1913 flood. *Courtesy of Dayton Metro Library.*

Fairborn), Brown began to lose her vision at age six and was completely blind by eleven. After completing high school at the Ohio School for the Blind in Columbus, she came back to Dayton and worked in a paper box factory. But she yearned for further education, and in 1911, with $93 saved up, she convinced a skeptical Ohio State administration to admit her to the

122

university. She went on to earn her degree in just three and a half years, becoming the first blind person to graduate from Ohio State. Afterward, Brown took her position at Steele, where she taught Latin, German, world history and American history. Her blindness hardly held her back, as she was said to have run a disciplined classroom—she even perplexed many students by demanding they take out their chewing gum, which they surely thought would go undetected. "They always smack so loud when they chew I can hear it," Brown explained. "I can smell it too."[127] In 1922, Brown took a sabbatical and went to Columbia University in New York City to earn a master's degree. In the 1930s, she returned to get her PhD. She then stayed at Steele until it closed in 1940, at which point she moved to Wilbur Wright High School to continue teaching until her retirement in 1952.

Steele High School's rival in football for many years was Stivers, and games between the two, usually held on Thanksgiving Day, were so popular that they were moved to the University of Dayton's Baujan Field, which has since been converted to use as a soccer-specific stadium after the football team moved to Welcome Stadium in 1974.

Steele High School, located very near to the Great Miami River, suffered major damage during the 1913 flood. Leo the Lion was also injured, as his base was destroyed and his tail broken. Funds were raised to fix Leo, and the statue was reinstalled the following year, but in the following decades, Steele as a whole began to decline. The enormous structure was expensive to maintain, and the abundance of wood used in the interior and the towers' wooden joists led to it being condemned as a safety hazard.[128] It closed to students in 1940 and sat vacant for years. The Board of Education put the building up for sale at auction in July 1953, but it was demolished in 1955 to accommodate a new Rike's parking garage. Some Steele alumni were reportedly so upset at losing their old school building that, for years, they refused to park in the garage. Fortunately, Leo the Lion survived the demolition and was moved across the river to the Dayton Art Institute, where he still stands guard today. The glassy Caresource tower has replaced the parking garage, bringing hundreds of office workers to the picturesque location overlooking the Great Miami River.

ROOSEVELT HIGH SCHOOL

Roosevelt High School, which stood at 2013 West Third Street, was an imposing building. At the time of its construction in 1923, it was said to be the largest high school east of the Mississippi, with four floors, over four hundred rooms and capacity for some 2,500 students. Roosevelt occupied two full city blocks, and its corridors stretched to a distance of one and a half miles. Its total square footage of over 300,000 was practically unheard of during those years. Amenities were plentiful, including a theater, two swimming pools, two gymnasiums, an indoor track, a greenhouse and a library with room for five thousand books. Roosevelt's architectural details were ornate and of the highest quality, and one observer called the school "exemplary of an era when fine marble and original artists could be incorporated into public buildings without an outcry of unnecessary expense."[129] Roosevelt quickly earned a reputation as one of the most prestigious schools in the Midwest.[130]

Roosevelt was named for President Theodore Roosevelt, which inspired its mascot of the teddy bear. The athletic teams were the "Mighty Teddies," and for some graduates, the teddy bear was such an important part of Roosevelt's identity that they adopted the hobby of collecting teddy bears for the rest of their lives.[131]

Race was also a constant issue at Roosevelt. At the time of its construction, the area around Roosevelt had been predominantly white, but demographic change on the west side of Dayton was significant in the following years.

Roosevelt High School was the largest high school east of the Mississippi when it was built in 1923. *Courtesy of Dayton Metro Library.*

Black Roosevelt students encountered segregation, as the environment was one that embodied a separate but equal doctrine, even though Ohio had had a civil rights law on the books since 1884. Roosevelt, in particular, had separate swimming pools (with the black pool far inferior) and separate dressing rooms, and blacks and whites even had their own sections for graduating class photos in the school yearbook. Blacks were also denied entry into the school's honor society.[132] Given this environment, several black groups began pushing for the establishment of black-only schools with black teachers, and this contributed to the opening of Dunbar High School in 1933 on South Summit Street. At the time, all the black pupils in the city were allowed to transfer to the new school. Nevertheless, many black and white students still built friendships together over the years despite the prevailing racist attitudes.[133] The west side continued to shift demographically in the following years, and Roosevelt was one-third black in the 1950s and became almost exclusively black by the 1960s.

Roosevelt had a storied sports tradition. Just as Steele and Stivers were major rivals across town, Roosevelt's major competition consisted of the other two predominantly black schools, Dunbar High School and Roth High School, which had opened on Hoover Avenue in 1959. The Roosevelt basketball team was one of the best in the state for a number of years, and it featured players such as Norman "Junior" Lee, who would go on to play for the Harlem Globetrotters for ten years after graduation. In 1960, senior Ray Brown was voted the Associated Press number one class AA player in Ohio. In football, Roosevelt grad John Henderson would go on to be the leading receiver in 1970's Super Bowl IV for the Minnesota Vikings.

Roosevelt also had a strong music program, which influenced many Dayton bands and contributed to the city's funk music legacy. Music teacher and choir director Charles Spencer made music theory a prerequisite for participation in his choir, and his devotion to his students had a major impact on Dayton funk bands in the 1970s.[134] Dayton has been called the "Land of Funk" for its scene during the years from 1975 to the early 1980s, as a "disproportionately large number of funk bands recording with major labels came from Dayton,"[135] among them the Ohio Players, Slave, Lakeside, Roger and Zapp, Sun, Faze-O, Platypus, Dayton, Shadow, Junie and Heatwave. Just about every one of the big bands had at least one member who was inspired by Spencer's teaching at Roosevelt. In addition

Coach Johnny Woolums and the Roosevelt High basketball team receive a warm sendoff as they head to Columbus for the state tournament in 1960. *Courtesy of Wright State University Libraries.*

to those who made it big, numerous other local bands earned a significant following more locally near Dayton, and countless musicians honed their craft with their lessons at Roosevelt, as well as the other black-majority high schools—Roth, Dunbar and also Jefferson High in Jefferson Township, a black-majority suburb. Samples from Dayton funk bands have also been used in major hip-hop songs from the 1990s to the present day.

In the 1970s, court-ordered busing plans were instituted in Dayton in order to achieve desegregation, and this had major implications for Dayton's black-majority schools. Many Dunbar and Roth students were reassigned to white-majority schools on the east side, and Roosevelt closed in 1975. In subsequent years, the building was used as Dayton Public Schools offices, a police headquarters for the Third District and classes for Central State University. When the school board leased school space to the city and renovated it at a cost of $1 million, it was called "one of the best things to happen in West Dayton in 20 years."[136] But the surrounding neighborhoods continued to decline rather than rebound as anticipated. Then, in May 2003, the school board voted to move its administrative offices downtown to Ludlow Street in the former Reynolds and Reynolds Building, a move that significantly emptied out the massive Roosevelt building.

In the following years, several groups proposed reuse projects that would have saved Roosevelt. In 2003, a group intended to buy the building and convert it to a mixed-use facility, including everything from job training facilities to a theater and a farmers' market.[137] In 2005, developer Karrington-Wilkinson announced a redevelopment plan that was also mixed-use, featuring housing, business space and social service agencies.

Many neighborhood residents pushed for preservation, citing the school's significance and the important role it played in the civil rights era in Dayton. Some activists compared the plight of Roosevelt to the case of Stivers High School, an even older building in a predominantly white area that was successfully being restored largely due to the efforts of a group of parents. (Stivers, however, was still functioning as a school.)

But in the end, none of the reuse proposals were deemed acceptable by the school board, and a different project ended up getting the green light. This proposal was to demolish the old Roosevelt and replace it with a new 120,000-square-foot building that would jointly house a new school and a community recreation center.

The building's demolition was a slow process, which was demoralizing for its advocates. On April 26, 2008, a group of two hundred alumni and supporters gathered at the school to tell stories about Roosevelt and sing beloved school songs. Above them loomed a massive crane that had already gutted the school of its decorative stonework. Some activists continued to fight and attempted to obtain an injunction to stop the demolition work—but to no avail. Roosevelt was completely demolished by the end of the year.

During the demolition, a time capsule from 1923 was found, and its contents were digitized and archived as the Roosevelt Historical Collection. Fortunately, the new Dayton Boys Academy and Rec Plex did retain some architectural elements from the lost Roosevelt School. And the land outside the school has been given the name Roosevelt Commons and features some of the pieces taken from the school's stone façade embedded in the ground.[138]

PART VI

DOWNTOWN:
THE HEART OF THE CITY

20

AUDITORIUM/STATE THEATER

Dayton's arts scene is impressive for a midsized city, and it's been ranked higher than many much larger cities.[139] Contemporary performing arts venues include the Victoria Theater, the Loft Theater and the Schuster Center for the Performing Arts on Main Street. But in Dayton's heyday, there were countless destinations, large and small, where people could enjoy a night out and a show. These were located all over downtown—Loew's, Keith's, the Strand, the Colonial and more—as well as in the surrounding neighborhoods, such as the Classic and Palace Theaters on the West Side. But two theaters in particular stood in relative proximity in a several-block area of downtown that is completely gone today.

The first of these theaters was called the Auditorium, but the castle-like building that stood at 32 East Fourth Street was originally the home of the Dayton YMCA. YMCA secretary David Sinclair, a Scottish immigrant, called it "the finest building West of the Alleghenies" after it was constructed, and in 1887, he launched the Evening Educational Program of the Dayton YMCA, which taught such subjects as bookkeeping and mechanical drawing. This would eventually turn into Sinclair Community College, which has been a downtown mainstay ever since.

Although David Sinclair had declared that the building would serve as home to the YMCA for fifty years, by just 1908, the Y and college had grown rapidly and departed for more spacious accommodations at 101 West Third Street, which is today's city hall. That year, the old building transitioned to a theater when it was purchased by Leopold Rauh.

The State Theater was originally a YMCA, as well as the first location of Sinclair Community College. *Courtesy of Dayton Metro Library.*

The new theater offered the experience of "talkie" films before the technology had even been invented, as actors hidden behind the screen voiced the action that was occurring.

In 1915, theater manager Gilbert Burrows was frustrated by the fact that theaters were not allowed to open on Sundays, so he decided to open the Auditorium anyway. He was promptly arrested, but the message didn't stick, as he tried again each of the next two weeks. After he was arrested on those two Sundays, a court appearance was imposed. That was enough to finally get Burrows's attention, but instead of caving in—facing his fine or possible jail time—he doubled down and "hired a gospel-singing family to perform the following Sunday, followed by a movie with a religious theme." The judge not only declined to punish Burrows for his crime, but he also permitted the theater to stay open on future Sundays.[140]

In 1923, the theater was renamed the State Theater after a change in management, and a decade later, RKO was added to the name after the company was bought by the RKO theater chain. It featured a lineup of B movies and did well through the 1940s and into the 1950s. But during the latter half of the 1950s, the theater declined in popularity, as was the case with many others in Dayton and across the United States during that time. Herb McClelland recalled that this was during the era of white suburban flight, and the downtown theaters often looked like "relics belonging to a ghost town." He expanded on his movie-going experience as a kid during that time:

> *Many a time I would enter the old State theater on Sunday to see a Frankenstein film or one of those silly but frightening prehistoric monster movies, only to discover that I was virtually alone in viewing it….Bats used to get in…and whenever they would fly in front of the projector, you saw giant shadows dart across the screen. It was eerie, especially during the showing of a horror film.*[141]

RKO bolted in 1964. A new company immediately swooped in and picked up the lease, but it didn't last long, and the State closed just a few months later. A movie house didn't seem financially viable to anyone by this point, so a new form of entertainment sprang up in its place: community theater. The plays performed in the same venue by the Dayton Community theater were successful, but they, too, would prove to be short-lived. This time, however, it wasn't financial troubles that doomed the operation but rather the City of Dayton.

GEBHART'S OPERA HOUSE
(PARK/LYRIC/MAYFAIR THEATER)

Just a block south from the State Theater at 22 East Fifth Street was another popular destination for entertainment dating back even further. Gebhart's Opera House was constructed in 1877 under the direction of William F. Gebhart and the "elaborately domed and galvanized iron front opera house was heralded as the finest to have been built in Dayton."[142]

The theater changed names several times over the decades; from 1889 to 1906, it was known as the Park Theater, when it featured live entertainment as well as the first movies shown in Dayton, in 1896.[143] In 1906, it was renamed the Lyric Theater after being taken over by a new company looking to create a classy vaudeville house.

Later on, it would change again, this time becoming a burlesque house. By 1934, it was known as the Mayfair. Burlesque star Ann Corio recalled one of her more prominent guests from that time: Elliott Roosevelt, son of President Franklin D. Roosevelt, who was stationed at Wright-Patterson Air Force Base. Interest in burlesque entertainment waned at the end of the 1940s, and the theater switched back to movies, but in the span of only a year, it returned once again to burlesque. The Mayfair shut down in 1968, and the building would not stand for much longer.

Old Gebhart's Opera House, as well as the State Theater, were directly in the path of a major urban renewal project. Back in 1963, city commissioner Dave Hall had proposed redeveloping the four-block area south of Fourth Street, between Main and St. Clair. A study at the time found that "the empty storerooms, the gradual deterioration of structural conditions, lack of maintenance and economic obsolescence of buildings has been apparent and is becoming more evident each year."[144]

Thus, all buildings in the four-block area, save for a Dayton Power and Light station, were razed in 1969. In addition to the theaters, additional casualties included buildings that housed furniture makers, jewelry stores, pawnshops and more, most with apartments above. Next to Gebhart's Opera House was Pruden's New Block, built in 1878 as the "first major commercial building of extensive size"[145] in Dayton. The theater itself proved to be a challenge, as it burst into flames the day before it was scheduled to be demolished, requiring nine fire companies to battle the blaze. The next day, a local union protested the demolition firm, claiming it favored Columbus workers when it could have used men from Dayton.[146] But in the end, the theater went down just like the rest

Gebhart's Opera House, later the Lyric and Mayfair theaters, sat on Fifth Street at the location of today's convention center. *Courtesy of Dayton Metro Library.*

of the buildings. The original renewal plan for the area was a mixed-use development called the Mid-Town Mart, including an office tower and retail alongside landscaped plazas and pedestrian walks.[147] After that plan was abandoned, a new one was put into place that eventually gave us the Dayton Convention Center, the Stouffers (today Crown Plaza) Hotel, the Transportation Center and the large green space of Dave Hall Plaza Park. Elevated walkways provide visitors added convenience but also let them completely bypass the sidewalks, sapping any vitality from the street-level experience. And just east of Jefferson on Fifth Street, the massive Transportation Center garage that connects above Fifth Street effectively serves to cut off the area from the nearby Oregon District. The spot where Gebhart's Opera House was built in 1877 is today the entrance to the convention center.

Gebhart's Opera House and the State Theater are long gone. But fortunately, the spirit of these smaller, independent movie venues lives on today in the same area that was originally cleared. In the shadow of the hulking concrete Transportation Center garage is the small Neon Theater, built in 1986 as Dayton's first new downtown theater since 1922. Even more notably, it was the first theater to be built in any major U.S. downtown area in over twenty years.[148]

ROBERT BOULEVARD

While a large number of buildings have been lost near the center of Dayton's downtown business district, the western side of downtown has seen an even more drastic change over the years. In this area, it is primarily residential structures that have disappeared, replaced by everything from surface parking to government buildings and one of the largest community colleges in Ohio.

The greatest concentration of these beautiful lost houses was on Robert Boulevard, once described in the *Journal Register* as "one of the most beautiful residential streets and parks in the country." Tree-lined and wide, with stately homes gracing both sides, it wasn't just a pretty street—it was a brilliant work of design and engineering. But it nevertheless proved vulnerable to Dayton's Great Flood of 1913, which led to its decline and later its eventual complete destruction during the years of urban renewal.

The creation of Robert Boulevard is owed to the perseverance of two brothers, Henry and James Robert, who hailed from aptly named Robertville, South Carolina. Their father, Joseph, a Baptist minister, was against slavery and moved his family to Dayton in the years just before the Civil War. James Robert became a teacher at Vassar before returning to Dayton to serve as principal of Cooper Female Seminary on West First Street, which is today the site of Westminster Presbyterian Church. Soon after, he became interested in a proposal by E.R. Stilwell, who founded the Stilwell-Bierce Manufacturing Company, to extend the existing levee to First Street from Monument Avenue. The river and the levee became a hot topic in Dayton, as the city had experienced several damaging floods during the early to mid-1800s that made their prevention a city priority. There was also a financial incentive: since many wealthy Daytonians had built their homes overlooking the river, success would turn the land along the extension into valuable real estate.

Robert, however, had an even grander vision: "He believed that more valuable real estate would be created by dredging the river basin and filling the land to the pasture that then served as a gypsy camp ground. The plan for his development had the plat extending from First St. to Fourth St. and from the Third St. bridge to the Dayton View bridge."[149] This is where brother Henry, a colonel in the U.S. Army Corps of Engineers, entered the picture. Henry became captivated by the project, and he would make frequent trips to Dayton to work on it alongside his brother. During these visits, he developed a relationship with Helen Thresher, daughter of the founder of the Thresher Paint Company, Ebenezer Thresher. They married on Christmas Eve 1860, which solidified Henry's presence in Dayton and his union with a prominent local family.[150]

Curt Dalton described how the job of creating Robert Boulevard was accomplished:

> *A steam shovel was used to fill in the area extending from First to Fourth Streets. Care was taken to make sure that elms, maples, and silver-leaf poplars planted by John Van Cleve in the 1830s were not disturbed. A limestone wall was constructed to retain the fill between it and the levee. Part of this wall can still be seen South of the Salem Ave Bridge along the river. On that land were constructed Robert Boulevard and Sunset Avenue. Park benches and iron urns filled with flowers lined the beautiful concrete walkways.*[151]

After an amazing amount of labor, the job was finished in the early 1880s, and Robert Boulevard would blossom into an idyllic part of the downtown community. Stilwell was the first to build a house on Robert Boulevard, and James Robert did the same on Sunset Avenue. For a *Journal Herald* reporter, "Robert Boulevard was more than a geographical site…it personified a way of life that reflected charm, culture and luxury at the turn of the century in the Gem City." But for James Robert, a sense of personal satisfaction would turn out to be the primary benefit he would receive, because although the project looked as though it would be a moneymaker, he didn't end up gaining anything beyond his personal investment.

Robert Boulevard met Monument Avenue near the Great Miami River and ran southwest, roughly parallel to the river, crossing First, Second, Lafayette (which ran between Second and Third), Third, Proctor (between Third and Fourth) and Fourth Streets.

After its construction, word started to spread about the wonders of the new boulevard, and Dayton's well-to-do began to build houses of their own there. In its heyday, Robert Boulevard exuded charm, simple living and a symbol of a Dayton that was flourishing and expected to do so for quite a long time. Jeanne Walters described a common scene in the *Dayton Journal Herald*:

> *The padding of horses' hooves, as they pulled fashionable carriages and their passengers along the boulevard, mingled with the laughter and the conversations of the promenaders enjoying their daily strolls. Gentlemen with high collars and jeweled stickpins escorted laughing young ladies dressed in long gowns with tight bodices and leg-of-mutton sleeves. It was a gentler time and a time when the fine houses facing the boulevard gave evidence of Dayton's stability and progress. The homes were built for gracious living and family life and, presumably, many generations would enjoy the life style of the original owners.*

Robert Boulevard was one of the most elegant streets in Dayton. *Courtesy of Dayton Metro Library.*

By 1910, nearly all of the lots had been purchased, but at that time, Robert Boulevard's new residents had no idea of what dangers lay ahead. The 1913 flood led many prominent downtown residents, many of whom lived on Robert Boulevard, to flee to the streetcar suburbs that sat on higher elevations, such as Dayton View and Oakwood. This also had a ripple effect on other sites explored in this book, such as declining foot traffic to the Dayton Arcade. In the following years, the homes were turned into boardinghouses or split into apartments, similar to other Dayton neighborhoods near downtown.

Today, the area surrounding the grand boulevard is a much different picture. Robert Boulevard met its end in 1964 when bulldozers "wadded to the one-time romantic walks and leveled the battered but still proud old homes,"[152] and the Brutalist architecture of Sinclair Community College, the Montgomery County administration building and other new buildings replaced them. In addition, I-75 cuts right through the edge of the area near the river.

Sinclair Community College, the Montgomery County Administration building and I-75 have taken the place of Robert Boulevard and other residential streets on the western side of downtown. *Courtesy of Sinclair Community College.*

Sinclair, of course, dates much further back, as it was founded in the 1880s in the location that later became the State Theater. In 1966, however, it shifted from a private junior college to a public community college. This was part of a major statewide push by Governor Jim Rhodes to create new state institutions of higher education. The new campus, located on twenty acres of urban renewal land, was designed by Edward Durell Stone, who also conceived the Kennedy Center in Washington, D.C. He came up with a unit of seven modern buildings with an open plaza in the center. The campus has grown significantly in the years since (it now has twenty buildings), but the original design is almost completely intact.

Monument Avenue, First Street and other nearby streets near Robert Boulevard and a few blocks to the east also once featured extravagant residences. One in particular, the 1890–92 Barney home at 239 North Ludlow Street near Monument, was called the most elegant ever to be constructed in Dayton. It was the home of Eugene Judson Barney, founder of Barney and Smith Car Company, the firm that had employed immigrants in the Kossuth Colony in the early years of the 1900s. A *Dayton Daily News* article described the home's luxurious character:

> *The red sandstone, Romanesque-style structure with matching stable held 27 rooms and 40,000 square feet of space. The interiors featured lavish paneling of rare woods, highlighted with pearl, onyx, marble and bronze ornament or inlay and tooled-leather wall coverings. The dining room looked like a luxurious Barney club car. Light poured through etched Tiffany glass windows.*[153]

In the late 1960s, the old mansion was operating as a funeral home, but it was sold in 1967 to a parking lot operator. Three thousand people turned out for a goodbye open house in April 1969, but the home was still demolished for a new parking lot. The Barney home's sad end has been cited as one of the catalysts for the growing historic preservation movement in Dayton in the early 1970s, along with the saving of the Burns-Jackson (Oregon) neighborhood.

A few old homes remain in this part of downtown. The Dayton Woman's Club, a Second Empire–style mansion at 225 North Ludlow Street, was erected by around 1848 in Classic Revival style and extensively remodeled in 1865. It was the longtime home of Robert Steele. The Dayton International Peace Museum at 208 West Monument was built in 1876 and was the home of Dayton businessman Issac Pollack. But this wasn't its original location, as the house was moved in 1979 from 319 West Third Street. Today, there is new residential construction, in the form of sixteen luxury townhomes known as Monument Walk, on Monument Avenue to reclaim some of the surface parking. These buildings may lack the beauty and splendor of the old Robert Boulevard, but combined with the Landing apartment complex (which includes the Spanish Colonial YMCA building) established in the 1990s, the western edge of downtown Dayton is once again a place that many people call home.

22

UNION STATION

Today, public transit options in Dayton are limited to buses and a downtown bikeshare program, and even the Greyhound station sits outside the city limits quite a distance from the city core. Dayton, however, is one of only five U.S. cites to operate a fleet of trolley buses, along with Boston, San Francisco, Philadelphia and Seattle. Although Dayton takes pride as the smallest city with this distinctive type of electric transit, it's one of the largest to lack a much more common form of transportation: intercity rail. What's more, there's no trace of the grand, once thriving train station that sat at Sixth and Ludlow Streets.

Union Station was constructed in 1899 at a cost of $780,000 and featured "a clock tower, a portico along Ludlow Street, five station tracks, and three station platforms."[154] Known as the "Tower Depot" due to the distinctive clock tower, it replaced the earlier "Round Top Depot" that had been built on the same location just west of Sixth and Ludlow Street around 1856.[155] Before that, a small brick building at Sixth and Jefferson served as Dayton's train station. The first railroad to come to town was the Mad River & Lake Erie, which began service on January 27, 1851.

The grand new depot came during a time in which many American cities considered it a point of pride to erect "large and architecturally imposing railway stations as doorways to the community."[156] Union Station's grand opening on July 21, 1900, wasn't quite as ostentatious as that of the Dayton Arcade three years later, but Daytonians were said to have danced in the streets due to their excitement for their new station.

The Tower Depot and tracks at Dayton's Union Station. *Courtesy of Dayton Metro Library.*

By the start of the next decade, Union Station had picked up in business, as over one hundred trains were coming through each day. This busy schedule led to some traffic congestion problems, but those were solved in 1931 when the tracks were elevated above the streets,[157] despite controversy from some Daytonians as the major project required a bond issue, and the nation was just slipping into the Great Depression. Nevertheless, the project went through, and the first train ran on the new tracks on December 15, 1930.

Since many families still lacked cars in these early years, train travel was a common and fairly affordable mode of transportation to other cities—even day trips to nearby locations such as Springfield. This made Union Station a frequent stop for both individuals and families for many more situations than just long interstate journeys.[158]

Visiting Union Station was a special experience for many Daytonians and, for at least one traveler, Elizabeth Stephens, one that engaged all the senses, including unique smells, "the scent of roasting peanuts, soot, and restroom disinfectant," and sounds, "the hollow sound of train-calls in the rotunda, the rumble of trains above, the shuffle of feet as the ticket-holders scurried about in last minute preparation."[159]

Dayton, Ohio., Interior Union Station.

The elegant interior of Union Station. *Courtesy of Dayton Metro Library.*

Union Station was such a hub of activity that many hotels sprang up in the surrounding blocks to cater to train passengers. The large Holden Hotel is one of the few old buildings that survives west of Perry Street downtown. Today, it is a public housing complex next to Sinclair Community College. Many other smaller hotels also lined the streets near the station, such as the Antler Hotel, which was so close to the tracks that trains passed only a few yards in front of it.

Dayton has been the site of many notable presidential visits over the years, and at least two of them centered on Union Station. In 1920, Franklin D. Roosevelt made a short speech at Union Station when he came to town to meet with James M. Cox, who was then the Democratic candidate for president, Dayton's only candidate ever to run for the highest office. Much later, in 1983, after the glory days of Union Station had long passed, President Ronald Reagan left from Dayton's Union Station for an old-fashioned whistle-stop tour across western Ohio. After flying into the air force base and giving a speech at Courthouse Square, he rode to Union Station, where he announced that he had to make a call but told the gathered crowd that they could listen. The call turned out to be to the crew of the space shuttle *Challenger*, and upon hearing the president say "Houston, Houston, this is Dayton," the multitude roared. This short presidential visit was called Union Station's "last hurrah,"[160] as by that time, it was already significantly weakened.

As was the case in practically all cities that once boasted of their train stations as markers of civic pride, demand waned with each passing year starting in the mid-1900s. In addition to declining usage, automobile traffic congestion again became an issue affecting Union Station in the 1960s. The City of Dayton wanted to extend Sixth Street through Wilkinson Street to help traffic flow downtown, but that was blocked by the station. So the elegant tower depot was demolished in 1964 and replaced by a smaller and much plainer version. At the rededication in September 1964, not many were dancing, unlike at the grand opening in 1900. And in the end, Sixth Street was later closed behind the convention center, so the razing of the iconic structure did not end up even providing a lasting improvement to traffic flow.

During this decline, however, at least one study explored the possibility of a new method of transportation for Dayton and nearby areas: a light rail line that would have connected downtown Dayton to its south suburbs. The proposal was made in 1973 when light rail was an emerging technology that promised to improve public transportation for all while reducing traffic congestion and pollution. The federal organization charged with supporting light rail projects, however, did not accept Dayton's initial proposal, and it was never resubmitted.[161]

Passenger train service was taken over by Amtrak in 1971—but with much reduced service—and the last train ran in 1979. The last remaining part of the newer depot was demolished in 1989. That same year, the majority of the tracks were removed downtown, and a decade later, Norfolk Southern acquired the remaining track through downtown. Today, freight cars along the elevated tracks near Sixth Street are a daily sight, but there's no trace of the once grand depot.

Some prominent mementos of lost Dayton buildings—such as the marquees of the Classic and Palace Theaters and the clock tower of the Callahan Building—were either saved by the city or acquired by Carillon Park. But you won't find the clock that once adorned the tower of Union Station. When the clock tower was demolished, the clock was bought by Wayne Avenue clock shop owner Warren Cron, who shopped it around to the city and the historical park. But finding no takers in Dayton, he ended up selling it to Balzer Tower Clock Company and Museum, located all the way out in Freeport, Maine.[162]

Passenger rail projects connecting Ohio cities, including Dayton, have been proposed in the years since, but none has picked up enough political will to move forward. Most notably, in 2010, the 3C Corridor project was awarded $400 million in federal funds as part of a massive stimulus package, but after newly elected governor John Kasich made killing the project a campaign priority, declaring that "that train is dead…passenger rail is not in Ohio's future," the money was revoked and directed to other states.

LOWE BROTHERS
PAINT STORE
(FIRE BLOCKS)

The Great Flood of 1913 destroyed much of Dayton with its sweeping waters, but for a bustling stretch of East Third Street, it was fire that proved to be the more damaging force. As the floodwaters spread through the city, the Burkhardt and Rottermann Drugstore on the northwest corner of Third and St. Clair Streets burst into flames after a gas explosion, and the fire began to spread. Burning material floated through a missing window of the Lowe Brothers Paint Store, drifting near an overturned paint can. The spilled paint caught fire, and the flames grew quickly, eventually swallowing up the entire block.[163]

The Lowe Brothers Paint Company traced its roots to Stoddard & Grimes, with John Stoddard branching out to manufacture farm implements and later automobiles. The firm assumed the Lowe name in 1872 when brothers Henry and Houston Lowe took over the original business and opened a small paint shop on East Third Street. In 1882, the Lowes took the business to the next level by establishing a factory so they could make their own paint. By the end of the decade, the factory occupied 134 and 136 East Third Street and consisted of a four-story building measuring forty by forty-four feet and containing a forty-horsepower steam engine, "paint grinders, mixers and other apparatus," as well as a larger four-story building containing the warehouse and sales floor. In 1890, the company employed about fifty workers including clerks and salesmen. The company grew and quickly became a nationally known brand, and the Lowe Brothers shipped their Dayton Ready Made Colors and Lowe Brothers's High Standard

East Third Street in 1899, less than two decades before it would be ravaged by flood and fire. *Courtesy of Dayton Metro Library.*

Liquid Paints to all parts of the country. In 1893, the company built a new warehouse at 452 East Third Street, which was soon followed by other facilities nearby.[164] The Third Street location's brick construction, however, would prove vulnerable to the fire that raged during the flood.

Observer J.L. Wilds described the surreal scene in a *Boston Globe* article: "The sight caused by the explosion of combustible contents of tanks, although of grave significance to us, was magnificent."[165] By midafternoon on that fateful day, five buildings on East Third Street—Finke Brothers, Johnson and Watson, Evans Brothers, Patterson Tool and Cooper Saddlery—had already collapsed, and the set of buildings adjacent to them were caught in fierce flames.[166] Roughly three hundred people were trapped in the block, and many of them attempted to battle the blaze. A group trapped in the Beaver Power Building at the corner of Fourth and St. Clair Streets "drew up water from the street in buckets, stored it in barrels and threw it on the building to extinguish cinders as the flock between Third and Fourth burned." Meanwhile, inside the factory building of the Ball Candy Company on Third Street, a group of over one hundred girls "emptied 300 candy pails and formed a bucket brigade to fight the flames" before they were rescued by a daring group that rode a motor boat into the chaotic scene.[167]

The Lowe Brothers Paint Company store and nearly all of East Third Street between St. Clair and Jefferson lay in ruins after the massive fire during the Great Flood. *Courtesy of Dayton Metro Library.*

After the fire was extinguished and the floodwaters receded, almost all of Third Street between Jefferson and St. Clair was completely destroyed, including the Lowe Brothers building. One account reported that when the fire hit the combustible paint, the building "exploded into oblivion."[168] The company soon rebounded, however, aided by the fact that it had factory buildings, warehouses and offices spread out in multiple locations. The Barney Power Block at the corner of Wayne and Third (next to the 1893 warehouse) later became the company's executive offices, with a major renovation completed in 1935. (Both of these buildings survive and are today part of the Cannery apartments.) The Lowe Brothers Paint Company went on to achieve even greater national prominence in the decades following the flood before ultimately selling to Sherwin-Williams in the late 1900s.

After the flood and fire in 1913, however, the buildings on and near Third Street needed to be replaced, and Dayton quickly responded by building new structures in the years immediately following the flood. New fireproof construction methods, naturally, were heavily preferred. The major player in this revitalization of the block was Adam Schantz, prominent Dayton businessman.

The first of the new buildings to rise was the Huffman Block at 111–29 West Third Street. Construction began in June 1914, and the four-story Chicago Commercial–style building was completed early the following year. A *Dayton Daily News* article praised the new modern building as "one of the handsomest and most complete structures of its kind in the city," with a façade of "fancy red brick [that] gives it an imposing and pleasing appearance," and its owners as having "contributed so materially to the advancement of the city and the development of its business section" so soon after it was devastated by flood and fire. The article also noted, crucially, that the new reinforced concrete building was "as near fireproof as modern construction can make it possible," unlike the old stone buildings that previously stood on the spot.[169]

The most impressive new building in the area was the Elks Building at the southeast corner of Third and Jefferson, designed by Dayton architect Albert Pretzinger. Built for the Benevolent and Protective Order of Elks, the building was dedicated by James M. Cox in November 1916. The

The Elks Building, the last to be built on Third after the flood, is today the gateway to the Fire Blocks. *Courtesy of Dayton Metro Library.*

Georgian Revival building was purchased in 1960 by Dave Hall, who would be elected mayor of Dayton five years later. Hall named the building Sam Hall Apartments after his son, who was an Olympic silver medalist diver. This is when the penthouse was added at the top of the building.[170] In 1986, the Elks Building was turned into offices.

The final major building to go up was the Dickey Building, just east of the Elks Building. Although plans to build it had been announced by Robert Dickey soon after the flood in 1913, it would take four years for construction to begin. After the Dickey building was complete, the block lost to fire had come back to life, with attractive and functional new buildings that demonstrated well Dayton's perseverance in the face of hard times and returned the block to a bustling business center. Although the block would lose its steam as the twentieth century progressed, like the rest of downtown, it nevertheless remained more intact than other buildings in an era when many were being removed in favor of parking lots or large-scale urban renewal projects. All of the major replacement buildings constructed after the flood survive to this day.

In 2015, developers Winfield Scott Gibson and Elliot Katz were exploring apartment conversions in the Huffman Block and Dickey Buildings. But after conducting more research into the Dayton market and its potential, they joined forces and added additional partners, greatly expanded their plans into creating a new entertainment district occupying many of the buildings on Third, St. Clair and Jefferson Streets. The proposed development adopted the name Fire Blocks. Due to the shift in scope and numerous financing delays, the project has taken a long time to get off the ground, but for a block that has seen so much over the years—from the earliest wood frame buildings lost to fire to the current buildings temporarily lost to abandonment—a rebirth would be significant for the city core.

CENTRAL MARKET HOUSE

D ayton had a public market occupying a central downtown location for over 125 years. In its early years, the market catered to Daytonians' daily grocery needs, with farmers arriving by horse and cart before dawn to set up their stalls, where they sold produce, meat, eggs and much more. In later years, the market house's upper floors housed important offices. The Dayton police made the second floor of the market house its headquarters in 1891. It was also Dayton's city hall, as the city never got around to building a structure dedicated to that purpose (and city hall's current location is a former YMCA building on Third Street).

The first market house to serve Dayton was built in 1815 on Second Street between Main and Jefferson. It was a modest frame structure that at first didn't even have floors. After it opened on July 4, 1815, the market kept hours of 4:00 a.m. to 10:00 a.m. on Wednesdays and Saturdays.[171] An 1816 city ordinance forbade the sale of staples, such as vegetables, butter, eggs and cheese, on days other than market days. (Meat and fish could still be bought any day before 8:00 a.m.) That year, you could buy a pound of butter for twelve and a half cents and a dozen eggs for eight cents, but a barrel of flour would set you back five dollars.[172] The already long market house building was added on to at least once, and by the next decade, it was clear that a rapidly growing Dayton required a second market house at a new location.

The location would be on Main Street just south of Third Street, as a long alley ran all the way from Main to Jefferson. At least one account described a "bitter rivalry" between Daytonians living north of Third Street and those south of it at that time, with the former group disparagingly calling the southern portion of the city "Cabintown." The proposed movement of the market house across the Third Street line prompted those in the northern half to strenuously oppose the new location, but in the end, the Cabintown contingent prevailed. As Robert Steele explained, "So bitter was the feeling that for a long time many persons refused to attend market at the new location."[173] The new market house was constructed in 1829, and the first location was shut down the following year.

Thomas Brown and Thomas Morrison worked together on the new market building project. After a decade, the new market house was expanded to run all the way to Jefferson Street. It remained an early-morning enterprise, but in 1838, the city attempted to hold market in the afternoon on Mondays, Wednesdays and Fridays, while keeping Tuesdays, Thursdays and Saturdays in the morning. The experiment proved unpopular, however, and shoppers soon returned to a routine of "the bell ringing at four o'clock…and the people hurrying at the first tap to the market house, as a short delay would deprive them of their favorite cut of meat or first choice of vegetables and force them to fill their baskets with rejected articles."[174]

The building was renovated in 1845, when the end was razed and replaced by a new structure, making the building flush with the street, and stronger pillars to support a second floor one hundred feet long and thirty feet wide were added. The market house then became known as the City Building, as it would house city hall, the police department and even the public library for a short time. In 1876, that building was torn down, and a new three-story structure was built at the same location.

A 1913 ordinance declared that the portion of Main Street in front of the market house "shall be used exclusively as a 'Flower Market'" and that the Jefferson Street side "shall be used exclusively as a 'Fish Market,' and no fish shall be sold at any other place in said central market."[175] That year, the central market had 38 butcher stalls, 52 vegetable stalls and 550 curb spaces. Butcher stalls rented for $175 a year, and other spaces went for $100.

The Central Market House declined as the twentieth century progressed, and it shrank to just twenty stands by the mid-1950s. At the same time, other buildings along Market Street were starting to be torn down for parking lots. According to Curt Dalton, "The first four stands were taken out to make room for a garage, then 14 were removed when the municipal court clerk's traffic section used the rear of the market. Supermarkets and lack of parking didn't help the sellers, nor did newer laws in meat inspection and milk pasteurization, which hurt the farmers who butchered their own meat

The Central Market House was also the location of city hall. *Courtesy of Dayton Metro Library.*

and brought their own milk to sell at the market."[176] The city closed down the central market house in 1956.

After it was demolished, there were several development proposals, including a city project that would have made the area around the old market a small shopping mall as well as new low-rise buildings to replace some of the surface parking. A restaurant on an upper floor would have overlooked the mall space.[177] After that, there was a proposal from private developers that would have turned the block into a "beautiful new shopping area." Some of this plan did get executed, such as a large new parking garage on the northwest corner of Fourth and Jefferson. The idea was for retail shops to fill in all of the first-floor spaces, which largely didn't happen, although the Cold Beer & Cheeseburgers restaurant later became a longtime tenant on the Jefferson Street side before moving out in 2014. After the parking garage phase, larger retail buildings would have been built, creating an area known as the "Mall Park Shops," which never materialized due to the larger decline of retail downtown. Instead, in 1966, the Mall Mark Motor (later Admiral Benbow) Hotel rose in its place on the Jefferson Street side, with a small park taking up the Main Street side. The hotel had a restaurant on its highest floor. It would last only two decades, however, before it would shut down. The 1970s and 1980s saw more buildings on the north side of Market Street demolished, creating a larger surface parking lot.

By the 1990s and 2000s, the central hub for Dayton's bus system was located at the corner of Main and Third Streets in front of the RTA offices in the American/Conover Building. Riders congregated at an open location right on a public street at a major downtown intersection. Frequent disturbances and drug activity led to a widespread perception that the area was unsafe for both riders and pedestrians passing by, and the *Dayton Daily News* dubbed it the "corner of chaos" in one of many media reports during that time. Many feared that the problem was significant enough to hinder any significant economic development in Dayton. Several solutions were proposed, including moving the hub to another downtown location near Sinclair Community College, to a location outside the city center, or even scrapping the hub system entirely. But soon a plan to re-envision the centralized downtown hub took shape that would utilize the former Central Market House space. The Benbow Hotel, which was abandoned by 1988 and later acquired by the City of Dayton, was demolished in 2007 as part of the hub redesign project. The RTA selected an architectural design from five options in January 2008, and a groundbreaking ceremony for the $9.6 million project was held on June 23 of that year. The new hub, called Wright Stop Plaza, opened on September 1, 2009, and today occupies the long stretch of the former market street in between Main and Jefferson. It features two bus-only lanes on either side of a covered island in the center for passengers to wait. The relocation reduced congestion at the corner of Main and Third, and arrests and crime on the site declined with it.[178]

In 2015, sixty years after the old Central Market House was torn down, a fresh food market returned to the site when the RTA and nonprofit Homefull launched the Market at Wright Stop Plaza, which offers fresh fruits and vegetables, a valuable service given that many bus passengers live in food deserts without easy access to healthy food. The market, located inside the plaza building next to the food court, is open year-round Tuesdays through Thursdays from noon to 6:00 p.m. The market also launched a grocery delivery service on bicycle for customers in the downtown area.

And a much larger public market experience can also be had just a few blocks away at the 2nd Street Market, which opened in 2001. The local food movement and growing popularity of farmers' markets in the 1990s led to an initiative spearheaded by developers Beth Duke and David Williams

The Central Market House location has been turned into the downtown bus hub. *Author photo.*

to establish one in downtown Dayton. The first version took place in the parking garage of the Cannery apartments. With proof that the concept was successful, it moved to an abandoned Baltimore and Ohio Railroad freight house built in 1911 on Second and Webster, where it thrives today. Despite the major shifts in shopping trends over the decades, and frequent knocks on downtown Dayton for not having a true grocery store, it's heartening that Daytonians can still shop for healthy local foods in the downtown core, much as citizens did over a century ago.

POST OFFICE

After Dayton was settled, pioneer settler Benjamin Van Cleve's cabin became the city's first post office (as well as the first library). After it outgrew that space, the post office moved around to nine different locations in the following decades, following a peripatetic path much as the public library did. The post office was next located in George Houston's brick residence on Second Street, the Winters Building on Third Street and the Beckel Building, among a few others. In another similarity to the library, the city was still in search of a permanent home as the twentieth century approached.

The U.S. government purchased the site at the southwest corner of Fifth and Main Streets and erected a grand new stone federal building there in 1892 at a cost of $150,000. But in contrast to the public library, which occupied its spot in Cooper Park for over seventy years, this elaborate post office wouldn't last two decades.

The early 1900s were a time when Dayton's rapid growth—its population nearly doubled from 1890 to 1910—demanded ever larger public buildings. In those years, the post office was a major operation. In 1896, the year of Dayton's centennial—when its population had just reached eighty thousand—the post office's roster featured postmaster John Ely and four other chief officials as well as a multitude of departments, including the money order department, the general delivery department, city distributors, a mailing department and forty letter carriers with six substitutes. Service had greatly improved since the early days of Van Cleve's cabin, when all mail was

The post office building at the southwest corner of Fifth and Main Streets was constructed in 1892 and demolished just nineteen years later. *Courtesy of Dayton Metro Library.*

carried by a post rider who came to the cabin only once every two weeks. At that time, Dayton was on a post route that ran from Cincinnati all the way to Detroit.[179] People from as far away as Fort Wayne traveled to Dayton to get their mail, and the recipient was the one who had to pay postage. At the end of the nineteenth century, mail was being delivered to Dayton residents two to four times every day, and outgoing mail was "repeatedly collected, both day and night from hundreds of street letter boxes."[180]

By 1903, conditions at the post office had become so crowded that public officials began to explore the possibility of expanding the building. But such a renovation wouldn't come cheap. In 1907, Congressman J. Eugene Harding introduced a bill that called for $325,000 to be dedicated to an upgrade of the post office. The bill was unpopular, but three years later, James M. Cox—congressman, *Dayton Daily News* founder and later Ohio governor and presidential candidate—amended the bill, saying that "what Dayton needs is a new, million dollar post office."

Congress eventually passed the new bill, despite some initial misgivings, and chose the southeast corner of Third and Wilkinson Streets, next to the Algonquin Hotel, to be the new location. Construction was halted during the flood of 1913 but quickly resumed after the area had been cleaned up.

The new federal building and post office opened in 1915 to much fanfare. According to one account, the building was "a public structure which bows to no one in the state and ranks among the best in the country."[181] Later, it earned the name "Grecian Lady of Third Street." The lofty proclamations of Cox were met, as the new eighty-thousand-square-foot structure featured "bronze ornamental panels in the lobby, furnished by Tiffany Studios out of New York City, that framed the service windows and bank of lock boxes lining the inner wall."[182] The exterior of the Neoclassical Revival building immediately commanded the attention of passersby with its ornate details:

> *The Third Street face consists of an iconic colonnade flanked by two main entrance portals. Each of the 16 two-story columns is carved from a single block of New Hampshire granite. The hand-executed ornamentation includes 91 lion heads peering down from the high dental cornice and a relief of an eagle, a pennant, and a wreath mounted above each of the two main entrances, the fruit of months of work executed by talented artisans of their time.*[183]

The old post office on the corner of Fifth and Main Streets was demolished in 1911, and eight years later, the twelve-story Fidelity Building rose in its place. The Fidelity Building once housed fifty offices for medical practitioners but now sits vacant after a burst water pipe in 2008 forced the eight remaining tenants to evacuate. It failed to reopen as planned the following year, and today, it is an eyesore along the southern stretch of Main Street in the central business district, near the Centre City Building. The city has sought historic designation for the building to aid its redevelopment, but the project has not picked up much momentum.

During the urban renewal era, Dayton's main post office moved to East Fifth Street in the area that was formerly the Haymarket neighborhood. The grand building on Third and Wilkinson was marked for demolition in 1975 after the remaining federal courtroom and various government offices relocated, leaving the building completely empty. But then the Dayton architectural firm of Lorenz & Williams Inc., which had restored other iconic Dayton landmarks such as the Victoria Theater (once slated for demolition), stepped in. The firm acquired the building with help from former astronaut Ohio senator John Glenn, and its restoration of the building was stunning. In the 1970s and 1980s, the building housed Lorenz & Williams's offices, art exhibits and event space. In 1994, part of the building was converted into a federal bankruptcy court, which opened

The 1915 federal building and post office. *Courtesy of Dayton Metro Library.*

the following year. The building still serves that function today and is still owned by partners at Lorenz & Williams, today called LWC Inc. Other tenants include the offices of Congressman Mike Turner. Although the Third Street building still looks impressive, many have forgotten that it originally housed the post office, and even fewer remember the short-lived original post office located on Fifth and Main.

NOTES

Chapter 1

1. Edgar, *Pioneer Life in Dayton*, http://www.daytonhistorybooks.com/page/page/1533813.htm.
2. Sanders, *Dayton*, 58.
3. "Central West," 215.
4. "Looking for the Dunbar House," Daytonology, February 13, 2008, http://daytonology.blogspot.com/2008/02/looking-for-dunbar-house.html.
5. Young, "Mrs. Hedges' House," http://www.daytonhistorybooks.com/page/page/5701206.htm.
6. McKee, *Big Town*, http://www.daytonhistorybooks.com/big_town_8.html.
7. Young, "Mrs. Hedges' House."
8. Chapin, *Urban Land Use Planning*, 311.
9. Dayton City Plan Board and Federal Civil Works Administration, *Housing Survey*, 5.
10. Ibid.
11. Ibid., 65.
12. Young, "Mrs. Hedges' House."
13. Konermann, "25,737 People Lived in Kenyon-Barr When the City Razed It to the Ground," http://www.cincinnatimagazine.com/citywiseblog/lost-city-kenyon-barr-queensgate.
14. "Who Are the Ahiska Turkish?" Ahiska Turkish American Convention Center Dayton, accessed October 10, 2017, http://ataccdayton.org/who-are-the-ahiska-turkish.

Chapter 2

15. Dalton, *Dayton Through Time*, 70.
16. "Our History," Oregon Historic District, accessed October 10, 2017, http://www.oregondistrict.org/history.
17. Bognar and Mays, *Oregon Stories*.
18. Merz, *House at 121–123 Brown Street*, http://www.daytonhistorybooks.com/f/The_House_at_121-123_Brown_Street.pdf.
19. Drury, *History of the City*, 589.
20. Nichols, Christian and Mayfield, *Dayton Album*, 103.
21. Oregon Historic District, National Register of Historic Places Nomination Form, December 1968, https://www.daytonohio.gov/DocumentCenter/View/386.
22. Bognar and Mays, *Oregon Stories*.
23. Ibid.
24. Burns Jackson Project Records, MS 142, Wright State University Libraries Department of Special Collections and Archives.
25. Bognar and Mays, *Oregon Stories*.
26. Kline, "Former Bar Now Has New Draw."
27. Breen, "Prediction Comcs Truc."

Chapter 3

28. "Classic Theater," Cinema Treasures, accessed October 10, 2017, http://cinematreasures.org/theaters/10070.
29. Owen, *Dictionary of Ohio*, 1,029.
30. Peters, *Dayton's African American Heritage*, 151.
31. Ibid, 149.
32. Dunham, *Dayton*, 74.
33. Smith, "Crusing the Nickel."
34. "Ted Ross, Actor and Gentleman," African-American Registry, accessed October 17, 2017, http://www.aaregistry.org/historic_events/view/ted-ross-actor-and-gentleman.
35. Smith, "Crusing the Nickel."
36. Peters, *Dayton's African American Heritage*, 183.
37. "Palace Theater," Cinema Treasures, accessed October 17, 2017, http://cinematreasures.org/theaters/20075.

38. Rodrigues, "West Fifth Street Renovation Planned," *Dayton Daily News*, February 6, 1996.

Chapter 4

39. "The Kossuth Colony Historic District," Ohio National Register Searchable Database, accessed October 10, 2017, http://nr.ohpo.org/Details.aspx?refnum=79001900.
40. Cichanowicz, *Kossuth Colony*.
41. Ibid, 8.
42. Zimmerman, *Hungarian Settlements*.
43. Cichanowicz, *Kossuth Colony*.
44. Ibid., 9–11.
45. Zimmerman, *Hungarian Settlements*.
46. Cichanowicz, *Kossuth Colony*.
47. Ibid.
48. Zimmerman, *Hungarian Settlements*.
49. Ibid., 86.
50. Ibid., 87.
51. Wilde, "What Happened To Hung-Town?," http://wyso.org/post/what-happened-hung-town-wyso-curious-goes-search-hungarian-dayton#stream/0.

Chapter 5

52. Friedman, "John H. Patterson and the Sales Strategy of the National Cash Register Company," http://hbswk.hbs.edu/item/john-h-patterson-and-the-sales-strategy-of-the-national-cash-register-company-1884-to-1922.
53. Martel, Bernstein, Martel, Heaton, Adams and Janning, *Dayton's Children*, 23.
54. Ibid., 24.
55. Chance, *Factory in a Garden*, 52.
56. Ibid., 130.
57. Bellaver, *Characters of the Information*, 142.
58. Mattox, "National Cash Register Successfully Establishes a Boys' Garden at Dayton, O.," 9.

59. Bond, "Electronic Ambush of the Stock Market," 324.
60. McClelland, *Daytonians*.
61. Martel et al., *Dayton's Children*, 25.

Chapter 6

62. "Making a Case for Delco," UrbanOhio, May 3, 2008, https://www.urbanohio.com/forum2/index.php/topic,16021.0.html.
63. Bradley, *Works*, 242.
64. Martel et al., *Dayton's Children*, 65.
65. Delco Products Division of General Motors Corporation, *Spark of Genius*, http://www.daytonhistorybooks.com/spark.html.
66. Wallace, "Water Street Development to Expand to Downtown Delco Building," July 1, 2015, http://wyso.org/post/water-street-development-expand-downtown-delco-building.

Chapter 8

67. Crouch, *Bishop's Boys*, 278.
68. "Wright 1905 Flyer," National Aeronautics and Space Administration, accessed October 10, 2017, https://wright.nasa.gov/airplane/air1905.html.
69. "Dayton Aviation Heritage National Historical Park," National Park Service, accessed October 10, 2017, https://www.nps.gov/daav/learn/historyculture/index.htm.

Chapter 9

70. Dalton, *Industries and Institutions*, 80.
71. McKinney and Isaacs, *Industrial Advance*, http://www.daytonhistorybooks.com/page/page/4923098.htm.
72. Billing, "Stoddard-Dayton Automobile Holds Historic Ties."
73. Kline, "Historic Structure Coming Down."
74. Carillon Historical Park, *Our Antique Autos*.

Chapter 10

75. Dalton and Roach, *Dayton Arcade*, 3.
76. Ibid, 19.
77. Ibid., 11–12.
78. Ibid., 22.
79. Ibid., 34.
80. Ibid., 65.

Chapter 11

81. Vasconez, "Kissing a Landmark Goodbye."
82. Dunham, *Dayton*, 36.
83. Nichols, Christian and Mayfield, *Dayton Album*, 36.
84. Zumwald, Christian, Rollins and Smith, *For the Love of Dayton*, 44.
85. Nichols, Christian and Mayfield, *Dayton Album*, 36.
86. Huffman, "Memories of Rike's All Warm."
87. Moss, "Local Tradition May Die."
88. Ibid.

Chapter 12

89. Ibid.
90. Drury, *History of the City*, 68.
91. Cummings, "Going Up?."
92. Korom, *American Skyscraper*, 321.
93. Young, "Downtown Clock a Reminder of '21 Competition."
94. "Under the Clock," *Dayton Daily News*, April 3, 1921.
95. Young, "One Good Clock Story Deserves Another 2 or 3."
96. Huffman, "Clock Marks Two Moments in Man's Life."

Chapter 13

97. Young, "Reibold Legacy Lives On in Building and Trusts."
98. Ibid.
99. McCall, "Reibold Getting a $12M Sprucing Up."
100. "Reibold Building," Emporis, accessed October 10, 2017, https://www.emporis.com/buildings/128335/reibold-building-dayton-oh-usa.
101. McCall, "Reibold Getting a $12M Sprucing Up."

Chapter 14

102. Dalton, *Industries and Institutions*, 86.
103. Watson and Young, *Dayton Comes of Age*, 42.
104. Johnson, *Field Guide to Flight*, 27.

Chapter 15

105. Hussong, *Home Amusement*.
106. Lakeside Park Advertisement, *Gateway*, 49.
107. Batz, "Lakeside History."
108. Dalton, *Dayton*, 93.
109. "Historical Geography of the Black West Side: Part III," Daytonology, February 26, 2008, http://daytonology.blogspot.com/2008/02/historical-geography-of-black-west-side.html.
110. Peters, *Dayton's African American Heritage*, 46.

Chapter 16

111. Dayton Triangles, accessed October 10, 2017, http://www.daytontriangles.com.
112. Collett and Presar, "Dayton Played Large Founding Role in NFL," Pro Football Researchers, accessed Oct 10, 2017, http://www.profootballresearchers.org/archives/Website_Files/Coffin_Corner/12-01-392.pdf.
113. Ibid.
114. Ibid.

Chapter 17

115. Faries, *Century of Service*.
116. Conover, *Some Dayton Saints and Prophets*, 262.
117. Faries, *Century of Service*, 13.
118. Ibid., 15.
119. Ibid.
120. Ibid., 16.
121. Dalton, *Made Do or Did Without*, 93.
122. "Dayton Metro Library," LibraryThing, accessed October 10, 2017, https://www.librarything.com/venue/12312/Dayton-Metro-Library.

Chapter 18

123. Young, "Memories from Steele High."
124. Dalton, *Dayton*, 76.
125. Watson and Young, *Dayton Comes of Age*, 152.
126. Conover, *Some Dayton Saints and Prophets*, 205.
127. Wolfe, "Dr. Brown Found 'Light' In Blindness," http://www.daytonhistorybooks.com/drbrownlight.html.
128. MacIntosh and Frame, *Craig MacIntosh's Dayton Sketchbook*, 44.

Chapter 19

129. "Roosevelt's True Worth Goes Unrecognized," *Dayton Daily News*, June 30, 2003.
130. McClelland, *Daytonians*, 66.
131. Huffman, "Roosevelt High and Teddy Bears."
132. Peters, *Dayton's African American Heritage*, 73.
133. "West Third Street Needs 'Roosevelt,'" *Dayton Daily News*, December 30, 2009.
134. Brown, "Land of Funk: Dayton, Ohio" in Bolden, Tony (ed.), *The Funk Era and Beyond: New Perspectives on Black Popular Culture* (Basingstoke, UK: Palgrave Macmillan, 2008).
135. Brown, "A Land of Funk: Dayton, Ohio."
136. Mong, "Reviving Roosevelt."
137. Kline, "Group May Buy Roosevelt."

138. "A Brief History of Dayton Boys Preparatory Academy at Roosevelt Commons," Dayton Public Schools, accessed October 10, 2017, http://www.dps.k12.oh.us/documents/contentdocuments/document_23_5_1099.pdf.

Chapter 20

139. Englehart, "Dayton Among Top Arts Destination Cities in Country."
140. Dalton, *When Dayton Went to the Movies*, 43.
141. McClelland, *Daytonians*.
142. Dalton, *When Dayton Went to the Movies*, 65.
143. Ibid., 66.
144. "Dayton: The Furniture District," UrbanOhio, March 26, 2007, https://www.urbanohio.com/forum/index.php?topic=12358.0.
145. Dalton, *Dayton*, 36.
146. Dalton, *When Dayton Went to the Movies*, 68.
147. "Dayton: The Furniture District."
148. Dalton, *When Dayton Went to the Movies*, 59.

Chapter 21

149. Walters, "Roads—Robert Boulevard," http://www.daytonhistorybooks.com/roads__robert_blvd.html.
150. Ibid.
151. Dalton, *Dayton*, 109.
152. Walters, "Roads—Robert Boulevard."
153. Kline, "Gem City Has Had and Lost Many of Its Gems."

Chapter 22

154. Dalton, *Dayton*, 25.
155. Rickey, "Dayton's Union Station," https://www.libraries.wright.edu/special/ddn_archive/2016/06/07/daytons-union-station-early-years/.
156. Watson and Young, *Dayton Comes of Age*.
157. Dalton, *Dayton*, 25.
158. McClelland, *Daytonians*, 10.

159. Ibid.
160. Nichols, "You Could Hear the Whistle Blow at Union Station."
161. "Dayton's Lost Light Rail Line…Set the Wayback Machine to 1973…," UrbanOhio, April 24, 2006, https://www.urbanohio.com/forum/index. php?topic=8612.0.
162. Nichols, "Museum in Maine Found Time to Buy Ex-Union Station Clock."

Chapter 23

163. Dalton, *Dayton*, 119.
164. Dalton, *Industries and Institutions of Dayton*.
165. Ronald, Copher and Ronald, *Dayton, the Gem City*, 100.
166. Eckert and McDowell, *Time of Terror*, 235.
167. Ronald, Copher and Ronald, *Dayton, the Gem City*, 100.
168. Williams, *Washed Away*.
169. "New Huffman Block Credit to City," *Dayton Daily News*, February 7, 1915.
170. Dalton, *Dayton*, 99.

Chapter 24

171. Drury, *History of the City*, 134.
172. Steele, *Early Dayton*, 132.
173. Ibid., 154.
174. Ibid., 172.
175. Bureau of Municipal Research, "Survey of Dayton Public Markets," 1914, http://www.daytonhistorybooks.com/surveydaytonmarkets.html.
176. Dalton, "Dayton's City-Run Markets Come to an End," accessed October 10, 2017, http://www.daytondailynews.com/news/local/dayton-city-run-markets-come-end/aRZm1sqViGHCOP4l8WZNDI/.
177. "From Market House to Bus Hub: 179 Years of Market Place," UrbanOhio, July 7, 2008, https://www.urbanohio.com/forum2/index. php?topic=16660.0.
178. "Reclaiming the Corner of Chaos," accessed October 10, 2017, http://www.popcenter.org/library/awards/goldstein/2010/10-20(F).pdf.

Chapter 25

179. *History of the Dayton Post Office.*

180. Ibid.

181. McGraw, "Old Post Office and Federal Building in Dayton, Ohio."

182. Gilliam, "History of the Old Post Office Building in Dayton, Ohio," https://www.dayton.com/news/special-reports/what-dayton-building-was-called-the-grecian-lady/jkEU1o4OWgsdZ5xJ7vKvPO.

183. "Old Post Office and Federal Building—Dayton, Ohio—U.S. National Register of Historic Places," Waymarking, accessed October 10, 2017, http://www.waymarking.com/waymarks/WMFKE2_Old_Post_Office_And_Federal_Building_Dayton_Ohio.

BIBLIOGRAPHY

Part I. Neighborhoods

1. Bomberger Park (The Haymarket, St. Anne's Hill)

Ahiska Turkish American Convention Center Dayton. "Who Are the Ahiska Turkish?" Accessed October 10, 2017. http://ataccdayton.org/who-are-the-ahiska-turkish.

"The Central West." *Library Journal* 42, no. 1 (1917): 215–16.

Chapin, Stuart F. *Urban Land Use Planning*. Urbana: University of Illinois Press, 1965.

Dayton City Plan Board and Federal Civil Works Administration. *Housing Survey, City of Dayton, Ohio*. Dayton, OH: Dayton City Plan Board, 1934.

Daytonology. "Looking for the Dunbar House." February 13, 2008. http://daytonology.blogspot.com/2008/02/looking-for-dunbar-house.html.

Edgar, John F. *Pioneer Life in Dayton and Vicinity, 1796–1840*. N.p., 1896. http://www.daytonhistorybooks.com/page/page/1533813.htm.

Konermann, Alyssa. "25,737 People Lived in Kenyon-Barr When the City Razed It to the Ground." *Cincinnati Magazine*, February 2017. http://www.cincinnatimagazine.com/citywiseblog/lost-city-kenyon-barr-queensgate.

McKee, Philip. *Big Town*. New York: John Day Company, 1931.

Morris, Terry. "Bomberger Center Sold for $831k." *Dayton Daily News*, April 26, 2012.

Sanders, William Leslie. *Dayton, Gem City of Ohio*. Dayton, OH: Dayton Daily News, 1963.

UrbanOhio. "Dayton's Urban Renewal Era…Part I…Intro and the Haymarket and vicinity." July 9, 2005. https://www.urbanohio.com/forum2/index.php/topic,4131.0.html.

Walker, Mabel L., and Henry Wright. *Urban Blight and Slums: Economic and Legal Factors in their Origin, Reclamation, and Prevention*. Cambridge, MA: Harvard University Press, 1938.

Young, Roz. "Mrs. Hedges House." *Montgomery County Historical Bulletin* (Summer 1967). http://www.daytonhistorybooks.com/page/page/5701206.htm.

2. Baker's Hardware Building (The Oregon District)

Bognar, John, and John Mays. *Oregon Stories*. DVD. Dayton, OH: 2007.

Breen, Sean. "Prediction Comes True; Wall Falls." *Dayton Journal Herald*, 1976.

Burns Jackson Project Records. MS 142. Wright State University Libraries Department of Special Collections and Archives.

Dalton, Curt. *Dayton Through Time*. Charleston, SC: Arcadia Publishing, 2015.

Dayton: A History in Photographs. Dayton, OH: League, 1976.

Drury, A.W. *History of the City of Dayton and Montgomery County, Ohio*. Chicago: SJ Clarke, 1909.

Kline, Benjamin. "Former Bar Now Has New Draw." *Dayton Daily News*, January 1, 2005.

Merz, Marguerite LeBreton. *The House at 121-123 Brown Street: An Oregon District History*. Dayton, OH: self-published, 1994.

Nichols, Jim, Marvin Christian and William Preston Mayfield. *Dayton Album: Remembering Downtown: A Stroll Down Dayton's Sidewalks*. Dayton, OH: Viewpoint Publications, 2004.

"Oregon Historic District." National Register of Historic Places Nomination Form. December 1968. https://www.daytonohio.gov/DocumentCenter/View/386.

Oregon Historic District. "Our History." Accessed October 10, 2017. http://www.oregondistrict.org/history.

"Steel Laden Cars Run Wild on Oakwood Line; Buildings are Smashed; Man Hurt." *Dayton Daily News*, May 14, 1918.

3. Classic Theater, Palace Theater (West Fifth Street)

African-American Registry. "Ted Ross, Actor and Gentleman." Accessed October 17, 2017. http://www.aaregistry.org/historic_events/view/ted-ross-actor-and-gentleman.

Cinema Treasures. "Classic Theater." Accessed October 10, 2017. http://cinematreasures.org/theaters/10070.

———. "Palace Theater." Accessed October 17, 2017. http://cinematreasures.org/theaters/20075.

Clark, Edwina. "Classic Goodbye is Set for Classic Theater." *Dayton Daily News*, October 6, 1991.

Dalton, Curt. *When Dayton Went to the Movies: A History of Motion Picture Theaters in Dayton*. Dayton, OH: self-published, 1999.

Daytonology. "Historical Geography of the Black West Side: Part III." February 26, 2008. http://daytonology.blogspot.com/2008/02/historical-geography-of-black-west-side.html.

Dunham, Tom. *Dayton in the 20th Century*. Bloomington, IN: AuthorHouse, 2005.

"Historic and Architectural Resources of the Mound-Horace Area, Montgomery County, Ohio (Dayton)." National Register of Historic Places Multiple Property Documentation Form. December 2000, https://npgallery.nps.gov/pdfhost/docs/NRHP/Text/64500484.pdf.

Huffman, Dale. "The Palace Guard—Committee of Two Trying to Save West Dayton Theater from Wrecking Ball, Return it to Glory." *Dayton Daily News*, July 7, 2000.

My Dayton Daily News. "Lasting Scars: The 1966 Dayton Riot." August 30, 2016. http://www.mydaytondailynews.com/data/special-projects/lasting-scars.

Owen, L.K. *Dictionary of Ohio Historic Places*. St. Clair Shores, MI: Somerset, 1999.

Peters, Margaret. *Dayton's African American Heritage: A Pictorial History*. Virginia Beach, VA: Donning, 1995.

RemarkableOhio. "Piqua's Early African-American Heritage." Accessed October 15, 2017. http://www.remarkableohio.org/index.php?/category/1099.

Rodrigues, Janette. "West Fifth Street Renovation Planned." *Dayton Daily News*, February 6, 1996.

Smith, Joanne Huist. "Crusing the Nickel—Remembering Fifth: In Days of Segregation, West Fifth Street Buzzed with Life and Energy." *Dayton Daily News*, February 1, 2004.

4. Kossuth Colony (Old North Dayton)

Cichanowicz, Stanley Raphael. *The Kossuth Colony and Jacob D. Moskowitz: An Experiment in the Settlement of Hungarian Immigrants in Dayton, Ohio.* Dayton, OH: University of Dayton, 1963.

Drury, A.W. *History of the City of Dayton and Montgomery County, Ohio.* Chicago: S.J. Clarke, 1909.

Dunham, Tom. *Dayton in the 20th Century.* Bloomington, IN: AuthorHouse, 2005.

Ohio National Register Searchable Database. "The Kossuth Colony Historic District." Accessed October 10, 2017. http://nr.ohpo.org/Details.aspx?refnum=79001900.

The Promised Land: Ethnic Groups in the Valley. Dayton, OH: Gem City Savings Association, 1974.

Wilde, Renee. "What Happened to Hung-Town?" 91.3WYSO, April 7, 2016. http://wyso.org/post/what-happened-hung-town-wyso-curious-goes-search-hungarian-dayton#stream/0.

Zimmerman, Elizabeth McKiernan. *Hungarian Settlements in Dayton, Ohio, 1900–1921.* Dayton, OH: Wright State University, 1979.

PART II. INDUSTRY

5. National Cash Register

Aeronautical Systems Center History Office. *Home Field Advantage: A Century of Partnership between Wright-Patterson Air Force Base and Dayton, Ohio, in the Pursuit of Aeronautical Excellence.* Dayton, OH: Wright-Patterson Air Force Base, 2004.

Bellaver, Richard F. *Characters of the Information and Communication Industry.* Bloomington, IN: AuthorHouse, 2006.

Bond, Winstan. "Electronic Ambush of the Stock Market," *New Scientist* 72, no. 1026 (November 1976): 324.

Chance, Helena. *The Factory in a Garden: A History of Corporate Landscapes from the Industrial to the Digital Age.* Manchester: Manchester University Press, 2017.

deBrosse, Jim, and Colin Burke. *The Secret in Building 26: the Untold Story of How America Broke the Final U-boat Enigma Code.* New York: Random House, 2005.

"Electronic Ambush of the Stock Market." *New Scientist* 72 No. 1026 (November 1976): 323-325.

Friedman, Walter A. "John H. Patterson and the Sales Strategy of the National Cash Register Company, 1884 to 1922." Harvard Business School, November 1, 1999. http://hbswk.hbs.edu/item/john-h-patterson-and-the-sales-strategy-of-the-national-cash-register-company-1884-to-1922.

Martel, Mark, Mark Bernstein, Kate Hagenbuch Martel, Lauren Heaton, Charles O. Adams and John Janning. *Dayton's Children: The Unlikely Gang Who Brought Us Aviation, "The Cash" and the Keys to the Road Ahead*. Dayton, OH: Engineers Club of Dayton Foundation, 2015.

Mattox, Captain A.H. "National Cash Register Successfully Establishes a Boys' Garden at Dayton, O." *Social Service* 5, no. 1 (January 1902): 8–13.

McClelland, H.L., ed. *Daytonians—Their Story*. Dayton, OH: self-published, 1992.

6. Delco

Bradley, Betsy H. *The Works: The Industrial Architecture of the United States*. New York: Oxford University Press, 2011.

"Delco Building." National Register of Historic Places Registration Form. May 2016. https://www.nps.gov/nr/feature/places/pdfs/16000462.pdf.

Delco Products Division of General Motors Corporation. *The Spark of Genius*. 1949. http://www.daytonhistorybooks.com/spark.html.

Martel, Mark, Mark Bernstein, Kate Hagenbuch Martel, Lauren Heaton, Charles O. Adams and John Janning. *Dayton's Children: The Unlikely Gang Who Brought Us Aviation, "The Cash" and the Keys to the Road Ahead*. Dayton, OH: Engineers Club of Dayton Foundation, 2015.

UrbanOhio. "Making a Case for Delco." May 3, 2008. https://www.urbanohio.com/forum2/index.php/topic,16021.0.html.

Wallace, Lewis. "Water Street Development to Expand to Downtown Delco Building." July 1, 2015. http://wyso.org/post/water-street-development-expand-downtown-delco-building.

7. Wright Company Factory

"Aircraft Production in Dayton: Wright Airplane Company, Dayton—1910." *NCR World*, September-October, 1970. http://www.daytonhistorybooks. com/page/page/4728770.htm.

Johnson, Mary Ann. *A Field Guide to Flight: On the Aviation Trail in Dayton, Ohio*. Dayton, OH: Landfall Press, 1996.

McCullough, David G. *The Wright Brothers*. New York: Simon & Schuster, 2016.

National Aviation Heritage Alliance. "The Wright Company Factory." Accessed October 10, 2017. https://www.aviationheritagearea.org/ wright-company-factory-site/.

National Park Service. "Dayton Aviation Heritage National Historical Park." Accessed October 10, 2017, https://www.nps.gov/daav/learn/ historyculture/index.htm.

Pruitt, Sarah. "The Fight to Save the Wright Brothers' Factory." November 14, 2016. http://www.history.com/news/the-fight-to-save-the-wright- brothers-factory.

Wright Brothers Aeroplane Company. "Dayton, OH." Accessed October 10, 2017. http://www.wright-brothers.org/Adventure_Wing/Expeditions/ Dayton_Ohio/Dayton_Ohio.htm.

8. Huffman Prairie Flying Field

Crouch, Tom D. *The Bishop's Boys: A Life of Wilbur and Orville Wright*. New York: W.W. Norton, 1990.

Dayton Innovation Legacy. "Colonel Edward A. Deeds—An Able Man Who Made Things Work." Accessed October 10, 2017. http://www. daytoninnovationlegacy.org/deeds.html.

National Aeronautics and Space Administration. "Wright 1905 Flyer." Accessed October 10, 2017. https://wright.nasa.gov/airplane/air1905.html.

National Park Service. "Dayton Aviation Heritage National Historical Park." Accessed October 10, 2017. https://www.nps.gov/daav/learn/ historyculture/index.htm.

———. "Huffman Prairie Flying Field. Accessed October 10, 2017. https:// www.nps.gov/daav/learn/historyculture/huffman-prairie-flying-field. htm.

9. Dayton Motor Car Company Historic District

Billing, Greg. "Stoddard-Dayton Automobile Holds Historic Ties." *Dayton Daily News*, May 29, 2011.

Carillon Historical Park. *Our Antique Autos: Carillon Park, Dayton, Ohio*. Dayton, OH: Carillon Park, 1982.

Dalton, Curt. *Industries and Institutions of Dayton Circa 1889: With Illustrations and Historical Information*. Dayton, OH: self-published, 1995.

"Dayton Motor Car Company Historic District." National Register of Historic Places Nomination Form. May 31, 1984. http://www. daytonohio.gov/DocumentCenter/View/384.

Drury, A.W. *History of the City of Dayton and Montgomery County, Ohio*. Chicago: S.J. Clarke, 1909.

Kline, Benjamin. "Historic Structure Coming Down—Structure Housed Auto Plant." *Dayton Daily News*, June 24, 1994.

McKinney, James P., and I.J. Isaacs. *The Industrial Advance of Dayton, Ohio and Environs—Historical, Statistical, Descriptive Review*. Dayton, OH: Groneweg, 1889. http://www.daytonhistorybooks.com/page/page/4923098.htm.

Rosenberg, Chaim M. *America at the Fair: Chicago's 1893 World's Columbian Exposition*. Charleston, SC: Arcadia Publishing, 2008.

PART III. RETAIL

10. Dayton Arcade

Dalton, Curt, and Nancy Brune Roach. *The Dayton Arcade: Crown Jewel of the Gem City*. Dayton, OH: Friends of the Dayton Arcade, 2008.

Dayton: A History in Photographs. Dayton, OH: League, 1976.

Nichols, Jim, Marvin Christian and William Preston Mayfield. *Dayton Album: Remembering Downtown: A Stroll Down Dayton's Sidewalks*. Dayton, OH: Viewpoint Publications, 2004.

Powell, Lisa. "3 Times Arcade Plans Got Our Hopes Up: Bingo Hall, Newspaper and Amusement Center." *Dayton Daily News*, April 7, 2017.

11. Rike's Department Store

Dayton Daily News. "I Remember Rike's—Thanks for the Memories." November 4, 1999.

Dunham, Tom. *Dayton in the 20th Century.* Bloomington, IN: AuthorHouse, 2005.

"History of Downtown Lazarus." *Dayton Daily News,* July 12, 1995.

Huffman, Dale. "Memories of Rike's All Warm." *Dayton Daily News,* January 4, 2003.

Kline, Benjamin. "Rike's Once a Jewel—The Store at Second and Main Was the Heart of Retail Shopping." *Dayton Daily News,* July 21, 1999.

Moss, Meredith. "Local Tradition May Die." *Dayton Daily News,* December 17, 1995.

Nichols, Jim, Marvin Christian, and William Preston Mayfield. *Dayton Album: Remembering Downtown: A Stroll Down Dayton's Sidewalks.* Dayton, OH: Viewpoint Publications, 2004.

Sharp, Brian. "Dayton History: Holiday Traditions." *Dayton Magazine,* December 2014. http://thedaytonmagazine.com/DM/Articles/Dayton_History_Holiday_Traditions_4293.aspx.

Smith, Suzanne. "Daytonians Mourn Loss of Spirit as Well as Presence of Rike's." *Dayton Daily News,* October 21, 1999.

Vasconez, Christine. "Kissing a Landmark Goodbye—Memories and Tributes Flow at Party." *Dayton Daily News,* November 6, 1999.

Zumwald, Teresa, Marvin Christian, Ron Rollins and Sol Smith. *For the Love of Dayton: Life in the Miami Valley, 1796–2001.* Dayton, OH: Dayton Daily News, 2001.

Part IV. Early Skyscrapers

Cummings, James. "Going Up? Last Ohio Elevator Operator Always Glad to Give You a Lift." *Dayton Daily News,* December 17, 1995.

Dalton, Curt. *Industries and Institutions of Dayton Circa 1889: With Illustrations and Historical Information.* Dayton, OH: self-published, 1995.

Dayton Daily News. "Under the Clock." April 3, 1921.

Drury, A.W. *History of the City of Dayton and Montgomery County, Ohio.* Chicago: S.J. Clarke, 1909.

Emporis. "Callahan Building." Accessed October 10, 2017. https://www.emporis.com/buildings/149125/callahan-building-dayton-oh-usa.

———. "Reibold Building." Accessed October 10, 2017. https://www.emporis.com/buildings/128335/reibold-building-dayton-oh-usa.

Huffman, Dale. "Clock Marks Two Moments in Man's Life." *Dayton Daily News*, November 15, 2006.

Johnson, Mary Ann. *A Field Guide to Flight: On the Aviation Trail in Dayton, Ohio*. Dayton, OH: Landfall Press, 1996.

Korom, Joseph J. *The American Skyscraper, 1850–1940: A Celebration of Height*. Boston: Branden Books, 2008.

McCall, Ken. "Reibold Getting a $12M Sprucing Up." *Dayton Daily News*, July 5, 1999.

Nichols, Jim, Marvin Christian and William Preston Mayfield. *Dayton Album, Remembering Downtown: A Stroll Down Dayton's Sidewalks*. Dayton, OH: Viewpoint Publications, 2004.

Watson, Claudia, and Rosamond Young, *Dayton Comes of Age: The City Through the Eyes of John H. Patterson, 1897–1922*. Dayton, OH: Montgomery County Historical Society, 2002.

Wright Brothers. "Bishop Milton Wright." Accessed October 10, 2017. http://www.wright-brothers.org/Information_Desk/Just_the_Facts/Wright_Family/Milton_Wright/Milton_Wright.htm.

Young, Roz. "Downtown Clock a Reminder of '21 Competition." *Dayton Daily News*, November 18, 1995.

———. "One Good Clock Story Deserves Another 2 or 3." *Dayton Daily News*, January 6, 1996.

———. "Reibold Legacy Lives On in Building and Trusts—Elder & Johnston Department Store Was Among First Tenants." *Dayton Daily News*, January 29, 2000.

PART V. RECREATION/EDUCATION

15. Lakeside Park

Batz, Bob. "Lakeside History." *Dayton Daily News*, May 23, 1993.

———. "Lakeside Lament—Construction of Roadway Draining Final Memories of Dayton Amusement Park." *Dayton Daily News*, May 23, 1993.

Daytonology. "Historical Geography of the Black West Side: Part III." February 26, 2008. http://daytonology.blogspot.com/2008/02/historical-geography-of-black-west-side.html.

Frolik, Cornelius. "Dayton Lake, Former Amusement Park Site, to Reel People in Again." *Dayton Daily News*, July 26, 2017.

Huffman, Dale. "Memories of Lakeview Won't Fade." *Dayton Daily News*, June 30, 1993.

Hussong, Nicholas Anthony. *Home Amusement c. 1880*. Dayton, OH, 1964.

Lakeside Park Advertisement. *The Gateway: A Magazine Devoted to Literature, Economics, and Social Service* 4, no. 1 (February 1905): 49. https://books.google.com/books?id=J5REAQAAMAAJ.

Peters, Margaret. *Dayton's African American Heritage: A Pictorial History*. Virginia Beach, VA: Donning Company, 1995.

16. Triangle Park (Dayton Triangles)

Collett, Ritter, and Steve Presar. "Dayton Played Large Founding Role in NFL." Accessed October 10, 2017. http://www.profootballresearchers.org/archives/Website_Files/Coffin_Corner/12-01-392.pdf.

Dayton Triangles. Accessed October 10, 2017. http://www.daytontriangles.com/.

Pendleton, Marc. "Howell Field Gets Makeover." *Dayton Daily News*, July 6, 2015.

17. Public Library

Conklin, W. J. "Public Libraries in Dayton 1805–1914." Accessed October 10, 2017. http://www.daytonhistorybooks.com/page/page/1781122.htm.

Dalton, Curt. *Dayton*. Charleston, SC: Arcadia Publishing, 2006.

———. *Made Do or Did Without: How Daytonians Coped with the Great Depression*. Dayton, OH: self-published, 2015.

Faries, Elizabeth. *A Century of Service: History of the Dayton Public Library, Dayton, Ohio, 1847–1947*. Dayton, OH: Dayton Public Library, 1948.

LibraryThing. "Dayton Metro Library." Accessed October 10, 2017. https://www.librarything.com/venue/12312/Dayton-Metro-Library.

Watson, Claudia, and Rosamond Young. *Dayton Comes of Age: The City Through the Eyes of John H. Patterson, 1897–1922*. Dayton, OH: Montgomery County Historical Society, 2002.

18. Steele High School

Conover, Charlotte Reeve. *Some Dayton Saints and Prophets*. Dayton, OH: United Brethren Publishing House, 1907.

Hackett, Brian, Dane Mutter and Gail Horvath. *Gems of the Greater Dayton Region: Special Places Reflecting the Miami Valley's Unique Natural and Cultural Identity*. Dayton, OH: Horvath Publications, 2007.

MacIntosh, Craig, and Robert Frame. *Craig MacIntosh's Dayton Sketchbook*. Dayton, OH: Landfall Press, 1985.

Nichols, Jim. "Hats Off to the Few, Proud, Steele High School Alumni." *Dayton Daily News*, October 4, 1995.

Sommers, Frederick Dickinson. *A Complete History of Steele High School, Dayton Ohio*. Dayton, OH: University of Dayton, 1949.

Watson, Claudia, and Rosamond Young. *Dayton Comes of Age: The City Through the Eyes of John H. Patterson, 1897–1922*. Dayton, OH: Montgomery County Historical Society, 2002.

Wolfe, Mary Ellen. "Dr. Brown Found 'Light' In Blindness." *Dayton Journal Herald*, July 22, 1964. http://www.daytonhistorybooks.com/drbrownlight.html.

Young, Roz. "Memories from Steele High—Pride Still Strong 65 Years after Graduation." *Dayton Daily News*, August 8, 2003.

19. Roosevelt High School

"A Brief History of Dayton Boys Preparatory Academy at Roosevelt Commons." Accessed October 10, 2017. http://www.dps.k12.oh.us/documents/contentdocuments/document_23_5_1099.pdf.

Brown, Scot. "A Land of Funk: Dayton, Ohio." In *The Funk Era and Beyond: New Perspectives on Black Popular Culture*, edited by Tony Bolden. Basingstoke, UK: Palgrave Macmillan, 2008.

Dayton Daily News. "Roosevelt's True Worth Goes Unrecognized." June 30, 2003.

———. "West Third Street Needs 'Roosevelt.'" December 30, 2009.

Huffman, Dale. "Roosevelt High and Teddy Bears." *Dayton Daily News*, August 23, 2002.

Kline, Benjamin. "Group May Buy Roosevelt—Former School Could Have Multitude of Uses." *Dayton Daily News*, July 11, 2003.

McClelland, H.L., ed. *Daytonians—Their Story*. Dayton, OH: self-published, 1992.

Mong, Cathy. "Reviving Roosevelt." *Dayton Daily News*, February 26, 2006.
Watras, Joseph. *Politics, Race, and Schools: Racial Integration, 1954–1994.* New York: Garland, 1997.

PART VI. DOWNTOWN: THE HEART OF THE CITY

20. Auditorium/State Theater

Cinema Treasures. "RKO State Theater." Accessed October 10, 2017. http://cinematreasures.org/theaters/6163.
Dalton, Curt. *Dayton.* Charleston, SC: Arcadia Publishing, 2006.
———. *When Dayton Went to the Movies: A History of Motion Picture Theaters in Dayton.* Dayton, OH: self-published, 1999.
Englehart, Laura. "Dayton Among Top Arts Destination Cities in Country." *Dayton Business Journal,* June 5, 2012.
McClelland, H.L., ed. *Daytonians—Their Story.* Dayton, OH: self-published, 1992.
Sinclair Community College. "Chronology of Sinclair History: Early Years 1887–1929." Accessed October 10, 2017. http://www.sinclair.edu/about/offices/archives/chronology-of-sinclair-history/early-years-1887-1929.
UrbanOhio. "Dayton: The Furniture District." March 26, 2007. https://www.urbanohio.com/forum/index.php?topic=12358.0.

21. Robert Boulevard

Dalton, Curt. *Dayton.* Charleston, SC: Arcadia Publishing, 2006.
Kline, Benjamin. "Gem City Has Had and Lost Many of Its Gems." *Dayton Daily News*, October 31, 1999.
Walters, Jeanne. "Roads—Robert Boulevard." *Dayton Journal Herald*, July 1978. http://www.daytonhistorybooks.com/roads__robert_blvd.html.

22. Union Station

Nichols, Jim. "Museum in Maine Found Time to Buy ex-Union Station Clock." *Dayton Daily News*, August 27, 2005.

———. "You Could Hear the Whistle Blow at Union Station." *Dayton Daily News*, August 6, 2005.

Reynolds, R. Kirk, and David P. Oroszi. "Dayton, Ohio Railroad History—Summary." Dayton Trolleys, http://www.daytontrolleys.net/drhs/daytonrailroadhistory.htm.

Rickey, Lisa. "Dayton's Union Station," Wright State University Libraries Special Collections and Archives. June 7, 2016. https://www.libraries.wright.edu/special/ddn_archive/2016/06/07/daytons-union-station-early-years/.

UrbanOhio. "Dayton's Lost Light Rail Line…Set the Wayback Machine to 1973." April 24, 2006. https://www.urbanohio.com/forum/index.php?topic=8612.0.

Watson, Claudia, and Rosamond McPherson Young. *Dayton Comes of Age: The City Through the Eyes of John H. Patterson, 1897–1922.* Dayton, OH: Montgomery County Historical Society, 2002.

23. Lowe Brothers Paint Store (Fire Blocks)

Dalton, Curt. *Industries and Institutions of Dayton Circa 1889: With Illustrations and Historical Information.* Dayton, OH: self-published, 1995.

Dayton Daily News. "New Huffman Block Credit to City." February 7, 1915.

Drury, A.W. *History of the City of Dayton and Montgomery County, Ohio.* Chicago: S.J. Clarke, 1909.

Eckert, Allan W., and W. Stuart McDowell. *A Time of Terror: The Great Dayton Flood.* Dayton, OH: Landfall Press, 1997.

"Fire Blocks Historic District." National Register of Historic Places Nomination Form. October 15, 1992. http://www.daytonohio.gov/DocumentCenter/View/370.

Ronald, Bruce W., Karen Copher and Virginia Ronald. *Dayton, the Gem City.* Tulsa, OK: Continental Heritage Press, 1981.

Williams, Geoffrey. *Washed Away: How the Great Flood of 1913, America's Most Widespread Natural Disaster, Terrorized a Nation and Changed it Forever.* New York: Pegasus Books, 2013.

24. Central Market House

Bureau of Municipal Research. "Survey of Dayton Public Markets." 1914. http://www.daytonhistorybooks.com/surveydaytonmarkets.html.

Dalton, Curt. "Dayton's City-Run Markets Come to an End." *Dayton Daily News*, March 9, 2016. http://www.daytondailynews.com/news/local/dayton-city-run-markets-come-end/aRZm1sqViGHCOP4l8WZNDI/.

Imagewerks. "The Cannery Lofts—Dayton, Ohio—The Development Story, 2002." Video, 12:41. https://www.youtube.com/watch?v=R9RKHH-_5vs.

"Reclaiming the Corner of Chaos." Accessed October 10, 2017. http://www.popcenter.org/library/awards/goldstein/2010/10-20(F).pdf.

Steele, Robert W. *Early Dayton with Important Facts and Incidents from the Founding of the City of Dayton, Ohio to the Hundredth Anniversary 1796–1896*. Dayton, OH: United Brethren Publishing House, 1896.

UrbanOhio. "From Market House to Bus Hub: 179 Years of Market Place." July 7, 2008. https://www.urbanohio.com/forum2/index.php?topic=16660.0.

25. Post Office

Gilliam, Tom. "History of the Old Post Office Building in Dayton, Ohio." March 1, 2017. https://www.dayton.com/news/special-reports/what-dayton-building-was-called-the-grecian-lady/jkEU1o4OWgsdZ5xJ7vKvPO.

A History of the Dayton Post Office from its Inception to the Present Time. Dayton, OH: Dayton Blank Book and Printing Co, 1896.

McGraw, Peter A. "The Old Post Office and Federal Building in Dayton, Ohio: A Case History of Restoration and Adaptive Use." *Bulletin of the Association for Preservation Technology* 12, no. 4: 55–64 (1980).

Waymarking. "Old Post Office and Federal Building—Dayton, Ohio—U.S. National Register of Historic Places." Accessed October 10, 2017. http://www.waymarking.com/waymarks/WMFKE2_Old_Post_Office_And_Federal_Building_Dayton_Ohio.

INDEX

ABOUT THE AUTHOR

Andrew J. Walsh is a writer and a librarian at Sinclair Community College in Dayton. His published works range from scholarly articles to web content and magazine features. He posts about Dayton history and development on his website DaytonVistas.com.